HOW TO BE A TRANSFORMATIVE PRINCIPAL

JETHRO JONES

JOHN CATT

First published 2022

by John Catt Educational Ltd,
15 Riduna Park, Station Road,
Melton, Woodbridge IP12 1QT
UK
Tel: +44 (0) 1394 389850

4500 140th Ave North,
Suite 101, Clearwater,
FL 33762-3848
US
Tel: +1 561 448 1987

Email: enquiries@johncatt.com
Website: www.johncatt.com

ISBN: 978 1 915261 09 0

Set and designed by John Catt Educational Limited

To my incredibly supportive family: Staci, Katya, Cali, Tenzing, and Eloise

For more information on how to get support for becoming a transformative principal yourself, please see
https://jethrojones.com/how2be

You can listen to any episode mentioned in this book by going to
https://transformativeprincipal.org
and entering the episode number at the end of that URL
(i.e., /episode386)

About the author

Jethro Jones is a consultant who helps schools and districts in the US to find simple solutions to complex problems. Named a Digital Principal of the Year in 2017 by the National Association of Secondary School Principals, Jethro has served students as a teacher, district coach, media and distance learning specialist, and principal, with experience at every level of public education. He has been hosting the *Transformative Principal* podcast since 2013 and is the founder of the Transformative Leadership Summit. Jethro is married and has four children. *jethrojones.com*

Contents

Introduction

TikTok Trend

At the start of the 2021–2022 school year, students had been out of school for as long as 18 months. All across the country, schools were scrambling to start in the midst of what the media called the third wave of the Coronavirus pandemic. While the adults were arguing about whether kids should wear masks, whether teachers should be vaccinated, and whether schools should offer a virtual option, devious children were making plans. It probably started out innocently enough. Kids hadn't been in school for a while, and although some may deny it, kids love going to school, seeing their friends, and getting acquainted in new ways. They know they feel safe in school and know that it's a place where they can often get the attention they desire. But, school has always been a place for practical jokes. We've seen trend after trend come through our schools and force us to make changes and adapt.

This new devious plan was even worse. The #deviouslicks trend on TikTok encouraged kids to steal or damage areas of the school, record it, and share it with friends.

Honestly, after telling kids that school doesn't matter enough to not cancel it, that their mental health doesn't matter because they can be shut out of school and their friends should be cut off because they coughed or had a sore throat, what did we expect?

Not only that, but we made (what I believe is the right) choice to not let school cancelations in the spring of 2020 "harm" any kids' grades. What kids quickly learned is a truth that has been since time immemorial: Grades are all made up anyway, and they don't really matter.

We told students that for the greater good, the things they care most about in school don't matter. As Chris Emdin said on Twitter: "Awestruck that adults cannot process that youth engaging in the deviouslicks challenge are expressing a need for belonging and care after a year of isolation and disconnection. We rushed them back to 'normal' without any attention to their mental health. What did you expect?" (2021a).

Recognizing the backlash, he later tweeted: "I am not justifying vandalism. I am recognizing that deviouslicks is a symptom of something deeper. It is a reflection of our shortcomings in 'back to normal' in an era where school is a trigger for the PTSD of interrupted socialization & child development" (Emdin, 2021b).

Our students, with all their extra time over the last year, have seen riots that destroyed communities, clashes of violence between groups, the hasty retreat of the world's most powerful army from a 20-year war, with people and billions of dollars in machinery and gear left behind, and many other societal issues that were addressed (or not) in their homes. Where we have typically had the school system as a brace to talk about these things as a group, in person, that was largely not an option.

And our kids suffered for it. Gaggle, an ed tech company that monitors student activity on school accounts for evidence of school harm, showed that in May 2021 there were many incidents:

> *"In every single major category Gaggle flags, incidents at the elementary level have increased by 100% or more:*
> *Suicide & Self-Harm increased by 191%, from 2.3 to 6.8 incidents per 1,000 students*
> *Violence Toward Others increased by 225%, from 2.1 to 7.0 incidents per 1,000 students*
> *Nudity & Sexual Content increased by 281%, from 0.8 to 3.0 incidents per 1,000 students*
> *Drugs & Alcohol increased by 317%, from 0.2 to 0.8 incidents per 1,000 students*
> *Harassment increased by 100%, from 0.9 to 1.8 incidents per 1,000 students"* (Railton, 2021)

How does this make you feel reading these statistics? Do you feel the frustration and anxiety that I do? Do you wonder about your own children and what you can do to help them not fall prey to these risky behaviors? I know I do!

Chris Emdin made a great point about us as a society not caring about student mental health. I will take it a step further than he did:

Safety is important, but as long as safety is the number one priority in our schools, nothing else is. I know that's a controversial opinion, but it's true.

If safety is the priority, then mental health cannot be.

If safety is the priority, then learning cannot be.

If safety is the priority, then education cannot be.

If safety is the priority, then relationships cannot be.

If safety is the priority, then culture cannot be.

You can only have one priority. Despite your best efforts. And believe me, I have tried.

The typical reaction to a problem like #deviouslicks is to create that policy and harshly punish anyone who engaged in it, often in the name of keeping people safe. In fact, we saw this in the fall of 2021, when the Department of Justice issued a statement about threats against school officials. "Threats against public servants are not only illegal, they run counter to our nation's core values," wrote Attorney General Garland. "Those who dedicate their time and energy to ensuring that our children receive a proper education in a safe environment deserve to be able to do their work without fear for their safety." I completely agree that violent threats against schools or school personnel should be investigated and punished if warranted, but this does not solve the problem!

In fact, in my mastermind group, one principal asked what she should do to combat the deviouslicks trend and other things like this. Although there were the typical suggestions of punishment, bribery, and the like, the conversation ultimately went to where it needed to go: proactive responses.

This was not the first trend that we had encountered, nor will it be the last. In fact, there were posts going around social media that shared different unsavory things to do each month of the school year.

Kids were making plans. In December of 2021, one of my mastermind clients reported that he had 151 of about 460 students out of school on December 17th because of threats made against the school in an effort to have the last day off before winter break! And his winter break didn't even start until the 21st!

Now, I'm not going to promise that this book is going to prevent these kinds of things from ever happening. I'm not going to promise that nothing bad will happen at your school ever again. But what I will promise is that if you implement what we talk about in this book, you will approach problems like the TikTok trend in a more healthy and balanced way, with an eye for the future and a way to build culture in a positive way so that people will actually think twice before resorting to whatever is trending. It's my goal to make positivity trend in your school, even when bad stuff happens. More important, I want you to be proactive, not reactive.

If your main focus is responding to the crises that come up, you'll only run around putting out fires. If, instead, you focus on proactive strategies as shared in this book, you'll find that there are very few crises that happen in schools. You'll start leading and designing your school; you'll be empowered to not see these little trends as end-of-the-world issues but simply as an indicator that we need to redouble our efforts in certain areas.

I know sometimes it can feel hopeless, and you may even think "I'll fix this next year." But here's the reality: It's never too late to make a change—even if it feels like it is.

The solution to this TikTok trend (and every other metaphorical fire in your school) is not to be reactive! The solution is to be a transformative principal.

Let's do this together.

How to be a Transformative Principal

Over the last several years, for my podcast (Jones, 2013–present) I have interviewed hundreds of educators: teachers, principals, superintendents, speakers, thought leaders. The list goes on and on.

At the end of each interview, I ask them, "What is the one thing that a principal can do this week to be a transformative principal?"

I've called this podcast, *Transformative Principal*, my PhD in educational leadership. With more than 300 hours of interviews, it seems like learning in dog years.

It's been incredibly fulfilling. I'll let you in on a little secret, though: As a principal, I was seeking advice right as I needed it. I used the podcast as my personal mentorship to help me learn how to be a transformative principal myself.

Here's the best part: You can use it for that as well.

The answers I received from the guests on the podcast were as varied as the guests themselves. The wisdom I learned from them was, and continues to be, inspiring.

With so many great leaders sharing the most important things to do this week, I've learned a few key points.

1. Culture is everything.

It will make or break whatever you are doing. But culture is elusive. You can't touch it. You can't point to something and say, "that's our culture." It's more of a feeling. You can point to something and say, "That feeling you have right now, that's our culture."

Some would argue that you can point to actions by others and describe those as our culture, but unfortunately they're wrong.

And here's where it gets interesting. Two different schools can DO the *exact same things* but have completely different cultures.

The challenge is that every school is unique.

2. Culture is about relationships.

The relationships that you have with your staff, students, parents, and community (and that they have with each other) are key to success. It's impossible to have good culture without mature, healthy relationships.

3. Good relationships require healthy, appropriate communication.

You'll notice I didn't say good relationships require everyone to always be happy and never disagree. In fact, the opposite is true. Healthy conflict is a huge part of good communication.

Now, if I were to write a book saying to do just those three things, you'd be in good shape, but I learned something else through the hundreds of interviews that I've done.

Culture is a BIG DEAL! It's so large, it's almost impossible to manipulate by focusing on it. Let's examine this a bit.

In their book, *The One Thing*, Gary Keller and Jay Papasan (2013) really emphasized the need for every single person to focus on one thing at a time. But it's about more than just focusing on one thing. They say that to achieve your goals, you have to focus on the right things. Too many times in schools, we focus on the wrong things.

When you have a messed-up culture in your school, your idea may be to focus on fixing the culture. This is the wrong choice.

In behavior management, we often ask, "What is the simplest thing we can do to change that negative behavior?"

In our schools, we need to ask, "What is the simplest thing we can do to change our school?"

That's how this book is organized. We're going to start at the simplest and smallest thing you can do.

Culture is the most important thing in a school, but you don't improve the culture by trying to improve the culture. You improve culture by working on the things that make up culture.

Keller and Papasan wrote:

> *Imagine a long string of dominos lined up one after the other, with each one progressively 1.5x larger than the last. If you were to knock down the first two-inch domino, you would set off a chain reaction that would, by the 57th iteration, produce enough force to knock over a domino stretching the distance between the earth and the moon. (2013, p. 12)*

Culture is the last domino, too large to move easily, but not impossible when you have the momentum building up to it by the other dominoes. In a great YouTube video, Dr. Stephen Morris (2009) demonstrates this by starting with a 1 mm × 5 mm domino. He started so small because the 13th domino in his example weighed nearly 100 pounds. Much bigger, and he wouldn't even be able to lift it himself (Bienaimé, 2015).

This is where so many other books out there get it wrong: so many books try to focus on moving the biggest domino, instead of the one that you can actually make an impact on. I'm putting the stake in the ground saying that the one domino you should focus on is self-care (Chapter 1). I've read dozens of educational leadership books, and so often, I walked away feeling that the amount of change was too big for me to do. In fact, many school leaders have told me they feel this way, and so many schools try to focus on the wrong things. Not only are they focusing on the wrong things, they are constantly changing the focus. In episode 457, Eric Makelky, principal of Pinedale Middle School talks about his three, never-changing goals. He says:

> *What can we do every year, year after year to make our school great and not change what we're doing as far as the focus? Number one most important to me as the principal is that every student who walks in this school has, and can identify by name at least one trusted adult. Number two, our focus as a school every year is to get better at reading and math growth. Our focus is to beat the state average for reading and math growth. Lastly, I think the hardest one, because it's new for a lot of people and I think it's also the hardest to tangibly measure is I want to demonstrate the beliefs, behaviors, and outcomes that create our school culture and improve our school culture every day, every week, every school year.*

Eric has learned the key to success. Clear, measurable goals that give people clarity on *what* we are trying to accomplish, with flexibility in *how* we accomplish it. But no flexibility on the *why*, because there is a clear vision that is communicated regularly. Eric believes, and his school needs, that the three things that will help them the most is kids having a trusted adult, academic achievement, and the culture of the school. Eric is a transformative principal. He is implementing what you will read in this book. I'm going to show you how to improve your culture by taking dozens of other small actions that you can actually manage.

The book is structured this way. Self-care is the small domino that you will keep coming back to again and again. When things are not going well, you need to make sure this domino is the one you are pushing.

As you learn to start taking care of yourself, start getting support (and have the power to give support) in chapter 2.

Then, start taking things of your plate: Delegation, chapter 3.

When you've got things off your plate, create a Vital Vision (chapter 4) for your school and for yourself. You may find that you are in the wrong school, wrong district, or wrong position to make that happen.

Once your Vital Vision is established, use observations (chapter 5) to assess whether that vision is a reality.

Then work on communicating effectively (chapter 6)

When you're communicating effectively, it will improve your relationships (chapter 7).

Good relationships, effective communication, a vital vision and all those other things will help you hire effectively (chapter 8).

By the time you are "working" on your culture (chapter 9), it will nearly take care of itself!

Truly, the way to be a transformative principal and change your school is to follow what I talk about in this book.

A few shortcuts to success:

1. You can only control you.
   Despite our best efforts, we can't control teachers, students, parents, school boards, superintendents, or anyone else.
2. What you spend your time on is what you value.
3. Our work must always focus on the individual.

Big data is all fine and dandy, but no students or families care about our schoolwide data if their individual data is no good. When 95% of our students have success the remaining 5% don't have success. They are 100% unsuccessful when we measure things that way.

So, here's how to read and implement this book. We know our big goal is to change culture, but we're not going to talk about that first. We are going start with the small domino, and build up to the big dominoes.

Early on in my interviews of other school leaders, I saw that culture would be the driving force that would help everything else. Unfortunately, focusing on culture alone doesn't actually work. It is all about dominoes. Culture is the big domino. It is the thing that, once you have a good one, will really move your school forward.

One principal recently said to me, "If I focus on culture, then it seems instruction goes down. Then when I focus on instruction, it seems culture goes down."

This principal was making a mistake that I have seen hundreds of school leaders make: She focused on building culture or improving instruction. It was a false dichotomy. While that doesn't seem like a bad idea at first, what she was missing was all the things that make up school culture.

Another principal came to me and asked for help in improving her culture. She kept focusing on big things, like teacher appreciation week and doing a lot of other work. She was letting other things slip through the cracks, like good communication, and more importantly, having a vision for her school. I asked her what her self-care looked like, and she responded that she was working 12- to 14-hour days and was exhausted all the time. She wasn't exercising and she wasn't eating healthily. I had to deliver some bad news: "You can probably fix your culture, but it will be really hard and take a long time if you don't take care of yourself first. People won't believe that you will take care of them if they don't believe you are taking care of yourself."

As you know, being a school leader is about so much more than just two things.

You may be thinking, "But I have to focus on culture!" I have heard many principals express a similar sentiment. When you think of the work you need to do to focus on culture, almost all of it is really focused on other things. You see, culture is something you feel more than anything. It is, however, not just something you can feel, but it permeates everything else. This means that it is made up of everything in a school. That's why the principal I was working with said culture falls when she focuses on instruction. The culture suffered because the way she was going about focusing on instruction was all wrong. Culture is linked to everything else. It's the big domino. If you try to knock it over without addressing the other issues, you're going to expend a lot of energy and not get very far.

Do you want to have less anxiety and stress?

Do you want to have time to focus on what really matters?

Do you want to build relationships that last, where you can still have the tough conversations?

Do you want to inspire students, teachers, and others to be their best, even when things are tough?

If your answer to these questions is yes, I'm going to help you do that through simple, effective, and powerful strategies all through this book.

I'm going to help you see that no matter where your school currently is, there is a simple and clear path to getting to where you want to be.

Through my mastermind, I've been working with principals from all over the world on these strategies since 2016.

Here are just a few very short success stories showing the domino method in action:

Gina needed to manage the transition to a new executive director at her charter school. She learned how to build the best relationship she could and brought a totally new person successfully into the culture by clarifying what was most important.

Kimberly made a goal to be more effective in her social media presence. After that, she won a district communicator award. Oh, by the way, she also won an award for improved test scores.

Trevor wanted to improve his instructional strategies in his school. He won a national principal recognition.

Nickie wanted to improve the culture in her school. She started out taking care of herself, and now has found a renewed purpose, her teachers appreciate her efforts, and she's found the courage to put people in the right places in her school for student success.

Greg wanted to help the middle 60% of his students. He managed the pandemic and has found how to help his principals level up in a powerful way, including bringing on a dynamic principal to replace a retiring 26 year veteran principal, who was capable of handling that difficult transition.

Margaret wanted to stop behavior problems happening in the lower grades in her elementary school. She's now the head of a successful international school in the United Arab Emirates.

Byron wanted to help more kids graduate his high school. Now he's the associate commissioner of education in Kentucky.

Whatever your challenge is in your school, whatever your anxiety is, whatever your goals are, the way to get there is to be a transformative principal. It's to recognize that your school can be in a better place regardless of where you are now, and you have the power to make it happen.

But what if you're not in that position yet? This book will also help aspiring principals start implementing the things that I'm talking about in this book in their current positions, whatever they are.

Teachers can start implementing these strategies. Assistant principals and deans can start here, also.

Finally, I have to say that I am not a quantitative researcher. I don't have quantitative data to back up everything I say here. What I do have is hundreds of interviews with successful leaders, as well as implementing their advice in the schools I have led. I find comfort in this comment from Patrick Lencioni, "But as Jim Collins, the research giant, once told me, qualitative field research is just as reliable as the quantitative kind, as long as clients and readers attest to its validity" (Lencioni, The Advantage, p. ix). Based on the feedback I have received from my podcast, the principals I coach, and my own experience, I can proudly say that if you follow the simple advice in this book, you will become a transformative principal as well!

Context Matters

Dr. Robert E. Quinn, author of the book *Deep Change* (1996), said that in order to improve our cultures, we need to start by learning from excellence. That's exactly what *Transformative Principal* is all about. There are hundreds of leaders to learn from.

At the same time, however, I've also had to recognize that what works for them might not work for me. And, I'm sad to say, it's not going to work for you either.

This is the important point: Learning from excellence doesn't mean *copying* excellence. It means that you learn from it. It took me a long time to understand the difference.

Dr. Byron Darnall told me that you can't just implement the same actions as others because context matters. You have to take what you have learned, apply it to your context, and find ways to make it applicable to your situation. Just because it exists doesn't mean it will exist for you. But here's where there is hope. Dr. Quinn said in episode 423: "If one [person's] doing it, that means it's possible." And that's all you need to get started!

It's not about doing exactly what others are doing, but it is about seeing that something is possible.

Let's bring this conversation down to culture. In your school, you may have an awful culture. In your school, you may have a great culture. It's probably somewhere in between. The lesson you *need* to learn is that it's possible to have a great culture, but it's not possible to have the *same* great culture.

So, as you read this book, what you need to recognize is that many examples are given throughout this book to ensure that you can see what is possible. As you read, ask yourself, "What I can learn from excellence?" Don't ask yourself what you can copy. In writing this book, I'm attempting to give you actionable suggestions that you can take and make your own.

Here's an example. Sam Sochet was appointed as principal of Martin Van Buren High School in 2012. The school was on the verge of being shut down, and the community wanted it closed. The four-year graduation rate was at 45 percent. There were a lot of Black and Brown students, and this didn't jibe well with the predominantly white community that lived around the school. Many people in the building appeared to not care about the school or about the racial divide that existed. Where do you even start with that kind of situation?

Sam's first public act as principal was to fix the clock that was situated on the outside of his building that had not been working for 20 or 40 years, depending on who in the community you asked!

Let's dissect this a bit and belabor the point to make the point. What you should not take away from this is that you need a working clock on the outside of your building. But as we read leadership books, that is often the takeaway: I need to implement this program or do things in this way. That piece of software is going to fix all our problems because it "worked" for that school over there.

Sam was faced with many intense challenges. And in his first public act, he made a very simple change. He fixed something that was a daily reminder of the failure of that particular school. Even more emblematic of the change he was trying to make was that he wanted to make meaningful change.

As he was meeting with his predecessor, a couple of students wanted to talk with him. They had two questions. One was whether they could have a football team. And the second one is incredibly insightful: Are we going to start wearing uniforms? Even high school students could see that context matters. They had seen other high schools taken over by new principals and saw that uniforms shortly followed, as a solution to whatever ailed those schools. They saw uniforms as the "magic" solution that other well-intentioned school leaders had made and that didn't actually result in meaningful change.

The point is simple, context matters. Without it, we can make gross generalizations and stifle change that we all need to make.

Let me end this section with one example where it made a huge difference. One of my coaching clients, who has been listening to my podcast for years, implemented some new ideas when she took over a school in the fall of 2020. Challenging times, for sure. She wasn't always popular, but she made some changes that were needed. They weren't changes that I would have suggested. In fact, in numerous coaching sessions, I suggested she was making the wrong choice. But she knew something that I didn't. She knew the context of her school. She knew what they needed because she understood the context of her school.

In February of 2021, she conducted an in-depth survey to see how things were going at the school. 83 percent of her staff and parents combined(!) said that her actions this year were "effective" or "very effective"! She had context, and because she understood the context, she was able to implement change that made a difference.

So, what is a transformative principal?

What is a Transformative Principal?

Transformative Principal noun. A school leader who inspires and helps others to achieve their full potential as human beings.

One of the questions I get a lot is "What makes someone a transformative principal?"

Dictionary.com (n.d.) defines transformative as "causing a radical and typically positive change in outlook, character, form, or condition."

So, a transformative principal is someone who causes a radical and typically positive change in their school community.

A transformative principal is someone who makes their school better. With that, change must happen. Change is rarely comfortable and must be approached in a way that will actually lead to success. The success is that the intended change is implemented.

But there is still more. The change must also be positive. And sometimes, a positive change to one person is a negative change to another. The transformative principal doesn't shy away from this and instead strives to bring everyone along. That's also not easy.

I also like to use *transformation* instead of *change*, because I like to relate it to the transformation that a caterpillar undergoes to become a butterfly. And here's the key. The life of a caterpillar exists so that it can become the butterfly. Its whole life is gearing up for that opportunity. Wouldn't it be crazy for the caterpillar to say, "I'm happy with where I'm at, and I don't need to change"? Of course it would.

This is how I feel about school leadership as well. It's not enough to say that I just want to ride this out and let the school be what it is.

Our purpose as principals is to make the school better than when we arrived. That's our purpose. Our purpose is to be a transformative principal and help shepherd our school through the change that needs to occur. Even good schools need to adapt and grow to achieve the full measure of their creation!

Each year, you get a new batch of kids, and no matter what you've done before, you must adapt to meet the needs of these kids. The need to transform is constant, and it ever will be.

But we don't need to be scared of that—we can just dive in and make it happen. In this book, I'll show you how to do that.

References

Bienaimé, P. (2015, January 29). *A domino the size of a Tic Tac could topple a building.* Business Insider. https://www.businessinsider.com/how-one-domino-can-topple-a-building-2015-1

Department of Justice (2021, October 4). *Justice Department Addresses Violent Threats Against School Officials and Teachers.* https://www.justice.gov/opa/pr/justice-department-addresses-violent-threats-against-school-officials-and-teachers

Dictionary.com. (n.d.). Transformative. In *Dictionary.com.* Retrieved October 27, 2021, from https://www.dictionary.com/browse/transformative

Emdin, C. [@chrisemdin]. (2021a, September 20). *Awestruck that adults cannot process that youth engaging in the deviouslicks challenge are expressing a need for belonging and care after a year of isolation* [Tweet]. Twitter. https://twitter.com/chrisemdin/status/1440007877305962496?s=20

Emdin, C. [@chrisemdin]. (2021b, September 20). *I am not justifying vandalism. I am recognizing that deviouslicks is a symptom of something deeper. It is a reflection* [Tweet]. Twitter. https://twitter.com/chrisemdin/status/1440009020945936384?s=20

Jones, J. (2013–present). *Transformative principal* [Audio podcast]. https://www.transformativeprincipal.org/

Keller, G., & Papasan, J. (2013). *The ONE thing: The surprisingly simple truth about extraordinary results.* Bard Press.

Lencioni, P. (2012). *The advantage: Why organizational health trumps everything else in business* (1st ed). Jossey-Bass.

Morris, S. (2009, October 4). *Domino chain reaction.* https://youtu.be/y97rBdSYbkg

Railton, L. (2021, May 25). *Our youngest students are not okay.* Gaggle.net. https://www.gaggle.net/blog/our-youngest-students-are-not-okay

CHAPTER ONE
Self-care

There is a vitality, a life force, that is translated to you into action, and because there is only one of you in all time, this expression is unique. And if you block it, it will never exist through any other medium, and will be lost.

Martha Graham

Put your heart, mind, and soul into even your smallest acts. This is the secret of success.

Swami Sivananda

Permanence, perseverance and persistence in spite of all obstacles, discouragements, and impossibilities: It is this, that in all things distinguishes the strong soul from the weak.

Thomas Carlyle

Thinking: the talking of the soul with itself.

Plato

Chapter Takeaway: Find what works for you to put your mental health, physical health, and spiritual health first, above all, because you deserve to be healthy.

We start with self-care because truly, of all the ideas and suggestions in the book, we have to hearken back to what I mentioned in the introduction: you can only control yourself.

Imagine your self-care as a three-legged stool. The three legs are mind, body, and spirit. Certainly, a three-legged stool is sturdier than a two-legged stool, but it is still precarious. It's still easy to fall over, so even if you have good self-care, it doesn't take much for that to get out of whack and cause you to fall over.

I'm going to go into a bit of a rant here. Most people say that you should take care of yourself so you have energy to take care of others. That's a recipe for disaster! And it's bad advice. We shouldn't have to justify taking care of ourselves so we can take care of others. We should take care of ourselves because we are human beings, and by nature of being human, we deserve to take care of ourselves.

I knew a principal once who became pregnant. She was so fearful that her work would be denigrated because she was pregnant that she kept it a secret. She was miserable. She worked longer hours than ever, took fewer breaks and sick days, cut off social connections, and isolated herself even more than a principal typically experiences. She was afraid that having a baby would ruin her career trajectory. She was afraid someone would be able to take her job because she was pregnant. Eventually, the secret could no longer be kept, but her paranoia and fear of others encroaching on her job had ruined relationships. People were very understanding, but she still felt fear and apprehension. She didn't take care of herself when it mattered most, when she was growing another human inside her. Thankfully, none of her fears came to pass, and her baby was born healthy and adorable. But, because she had distanced herself so much from those with whom she worked, it was hard to get back to where she had been. For the first few months, while she kept her pregnancy secret, people couldn't celebrate with her and support her. She robbed her closest coworkers of the opportunity to be supportive and caring. She robbed herself and her peers of the support that she deserved just because she is human. Not only that, because of the timing, she ruined many relationships that didn't need ruining.

You might think that story should have been at the beginning of the section on relationships, but her problem wasn't relationships. That was a symptom of her problem of a lack of self-care. She didn't do the things that gave her energy. She didn't take care of herself appropriately, and it caused her to go through some challenges later on. It stunted her career, it degraded her relationships, and it affected her school and her family—

everyone around her. While she wasn't taking care of herself, her stool became even more difficult to balance on, and the way she reacted was tough on her and those who cared about her.

We can trace many of our problems back to self-care. Here are a few more examples to help illustrate this.

In another situation, I knew a principal who was going through a faith crisis and had rejected what he believed in growing up and rejected the spirituality that he had believed had helped him get to the point where he was in his career, leading a school that would make any principal proud. Eventually, this man cheated on his wife with a coworker and lost the respect of his family, staff, and students who eventually also found out. Having an affair was bad, but I'm not here to judge that aspect. Again, what preceded the affair was not his lustful desires, nor was it a desire to separate from his wife. What led to his affair, the symptom of a bigger issue, was that he was not doing the self-care he needed for his spirit, because he had departed from what he believed.

A superintendent described the failures of a principal that worked for him as she tried to get better. He said it was too little, too late. He questioned whether she was capable even of learning what she needed to learn to be successful in his district. He didn't believe that she had the mind to learn what she needed. That is a damning commentary coming from someone who is the leader of a learning organization, right? While this principal had been a promising young first year principal, after several years at the top spot in a school, she hadn't grown mentally as she needed to. She saw herself in a position of "I have arrived." And that attitude of significantly slowing her learning after a hard-fought masters degree in educational leadership had led her to think, "I've put in all this work, and now I can relax and just do my job." She failed to realize that her job was to continue learning and growing. She attended professional development and did what she needed to, but in her slow movement, the district passed her by and she wasn't going to be successful anymore.

Finally, I'll share my own personal struggle. I was under an intense amount of pressure as a principal one year. I was incredibly stressed, and instead of dealing with the stress in a healthy way, I succumbed to overeating, not exercising, and not sleeping as much as I needed to.

Eventually, I contracted shingles on my neck and chest. If you have never had that, it looks like your skin is scaled, like a snake, and it itches and burns. It's incredibly uncomfortable. My body paid the price for my inability to deal appropriately with my stress. But again, it was not the stress that did it. In fact, as I look back, I was under greater stress later in my career as a principal, but didn't react in the same way.

Why not? Because I learned how to take care of myself. Taking care of yourself is vitally important. Whatever you think you may accomplish at work by sacrificing yourself is not worth the toll it takes on your mind, body, and spirit.

In many instances, you won't actually notice that one of your stool legs is the wrong length, until it breaks. It requires more effort and work to lose 50 pounds than to maintain your weight. It requires much more effort and work to dig yourself out of a spiritual hole than to maintain your spiritual stance. And it takes much more effort to try and cram knowledge in that last minute than to continue to study and seek knowledge throughout your life.

We will talk through each of the three legs of a stool in the next sections, but before we do, we have to recognize something that we usually use as an excuse: my work is important and if I don't do this, who will?

Schools are big, vast machines. And you, no matter your position are a cog in a machine. When you break, which you will if you don't take care of yourself, you will be replaced with a different cog. No matter how great you may think you are. No matter how much good you have done. No matter how much you have sacrificed. You will be replaced. You must be replaced.

You are irreplaceable, but you are very replaceable.

What I mean is there will never be another person like you, as referenced in the Martha Graham quote at the beginning of this chapter. At the same time, you are just a cog in a machine, and someone else can do the job in a heartbeat.

That means you should bring your best, whole self to work every day. There's only one way to do that: Take care of yourself.

Before we get into the sections about mind, body, and spirit, we should understand two important truths that relate to all three areas.

Inputs: What you put into your mind, body, and spirit makes a difference. Be wise about what you ingest in each of these areas.

Outputs/Exercise: Your mind, body, and spirit need exercise. Define what works for you and stick with it! What you do in each area matters. Writing, drawing, thinking, pondering, praying: they all have an impact.

An important aspect of self-care is pay attention to what your inputs are and your exercises are. You should have a plan for each in the three areas.

What will you put into your mind, your body, and your spirit?

What will you do to exercise your mind, your body, and your spirit?

Let's dive in.

Mind

Melissa Bernstein (episode 427) is the founder of the toy company Melissa and Doug. You know it right? Of course! Some of the best toys ever created that are high quality, beautifully designed, and also good learning tools. For the last 30 years, Melissa has carried a dark secret. She has struggled with depression. She's had a deep, dark battle with this horrible monster. However, the toy company was her salvation. She said, "Melissa and Doug was actually my salvation. Because when I realized with shock that I could actually create toys! I never thought I could create toys. I never studied to be any form of designer. And I never even really associated with being creative because being creative meant I was weird and I didn't want to be weird. I wanted to be accepted and popular and normal. Creativity just raged through me and created all this dark stuff that I never let see the light. So even though I created like for the first two decades of my life incessantly, no one ever saw it and it never brought me meaning and it stayed in darkness." She would write poetry to help her, but her poetry was always dark and people didn't like that. Especially not her teachers. You've seen that, I'm sure. The quiet, dark kids come across as weird and people don't like them as much. They are ostracized.

But, we all have dark parts of our mind that could come out in unexpected ways. For Melissa, being able to design toys was something that helped her be publicly creative while she continued to write poetry that was often dark and she could share it with those close to her.

Melissa continued, "It was the first 'dot moment' of my life, which was that I had a choice, whether to take that horrible darkness that just suffused me every day and either channel it into more darkness, through writing music and writing verses that were in my journals, which were just so dark or I realized I could take it and channel the very same angst into beautiful light, bright toys that could actually incite imagination and wonder in kids. And that realization changed my life. So yes, it did help me immensely. However, although I was channeling all the darkness into light, through making toys, I still wasn't accepting who I was in all the qualities that gave me the ability to create and make those toys."

There are three things we need to do to take care of our minds: learn, create, and reflect. I shared this story of Melissa because her story illustrates all three of these aspects so beautifully.

Learn is about keeping our mind alert to new opportunities for growth.

She didn't become a toy designer by going to school. She actually created light and beautiful things to combat the darkness raging inside her. She learned how to create beautiful things, and she reflects on her life and experiences.

Create is about doing something creative. Creativity is one of the most powerful things we can do. And creativity doesn't only mean painting, drawing, or other things we typically think of as creativity. Melissa Bernstein calls it self-expression. "I think it all comes in discovery and exploring what your innate sparks are. I think so much is put toward what society thinks we should be doing, like you have to play sports, you have to do these certain things you have to do well in school. that I think today kids are growing up, they're in high school and they don't even really know what makes their own hearts sing. We're talking about earlier and earlier having questions, you know, really digging deep and saying, what might I like to sow? What form of self-expression exists in my heart and I can sow those seeds and really find that thing that brings me joy and asking more questions. Do I want to give of myself? Do I want to serve others? I mean, there are a lot of questions you can start to ask yourself before you're going to college and you have no idea who you are. So I think the earlier we can find those gifts in us and what our self-expression language is, then we can really start to by that figure out what might we want to do in life."

Stay Out of People's Minds!

Your own mind is complicated enough! My wife has a life coach named Jody Moore, and she teaches people how to manage their emotions. Most of Jody's clients are women, and one of the most common things they talk about is moms trying to control their (especially adult) children's lives. Jody is constantly telling them to stay out of their kids' minds. To stop assigning expectations and blame to what they are doing. It's only hurtful in the end.

You can't control anyone, nor can you know what their reasons are for doing specific things. It is impossible. You can only interpret, in your own way, what you think they are doing. It's too difficult. When we assume positive intentions and stay out of their minds, it keeps us from trying to control them.

Staying in your own mind and improving there is how you take care of yourself. One thing you can always count on is that things change. Next year, you're going to have a new group of kids with new ideas about how they should interact with your school. They'll bring a different feel and culture to your school. Even if you got everything perfect this year, you will never have the same group of kids two years in a row. You must be ready for what you've done in the past to not work. So, learn how to do it better.

I suggest that learning should be constant for you. Following this framework for learning will help you significantly, it is a simplified version of what we do with kids every single day.

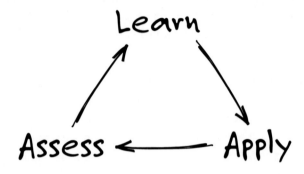

The model is to learn, apply, assess. It's quite simple, but if you do it every day, you will keep your mind fresh and up to date. Lest you think I'm talking about keeping your mind fresh on educational topics, I'm not. Your own personal knowledge is like a garden that must be nurtured regularly. The fruits and vegetables that you grow are your choice. It doesn't matter what you learn, apply, assess, just that you do it regularly.

As an educational leader, you should always be learning. Many principals call themselves the "lead learner" of their schools. When you learn something new, you should do your best to apply it. If you took all the answers from the last question I ask on my podcast, you would have more than five straight hours of suggestions for how to improve your school. That's a lot! If you've listened to my podcast since the beginning and implemented each of those suggestions over the last eight years, you'd certainly be a transformative principal, and you'd be a model for this approach.

Once you apply something, you need to assess whether or not it was worthwhile. Unfortunately, in education, we've made this too academic. It's really quite simple. Here's an example. Let's say you were reading a book about, oh, I don't know, educational leadership. And the author says something brilliant, and you say, "That's new to me! I should make a plan of how to implement that, call the leadership team and see if they think it's a good idea, then pull in the PTA and make sure we've got community buy-in, and then wordsmith it so that everyone feels good about it!"

No. Just stop.

Learn something. Apply it in the smallest way possible, and then assess whether or not it was a good idea.

Let's get a little more granular. Kirk Wheeler suggested to me in episode 424 that I should start a five-year journal. Sounds super overwhelming! He explained it this way: "When you open to a page, divide it up into five sections, right on one page, and there's maybe five lines in each section. And write down April 19, 2022 and you've got about five lines to reflect on your day. And I'm a huge believer in reflecting, connecting it to what your intentions were at the beginning of the day. We turn to the next page. The next day on and on. The magic happens when you come back a year later, and now it's April 19, 2023, and I'm writing in the second section. And then I moved through the year three, I'm writing in the third section. So before you know it, you are writing a section again, five lines."

Eventually, you're writing just a couple lines each day for five years. You can come back and see where your mind was each year on that same day. Some of these five-year journals have prompts, but I'm not really a fan of that. I like my creativity to flow however it sees fit.

So, if this is the thing you have learned, don't go buy a five-year journal. Get a sticky note and write it on there. Get a note card and write it on there. Apply what you've learned. Then assess whether or not you like it. That's exactly what I did. I started writing things down on a note card, and then thought, "You know what? I like this!" Now, I have a beautiful leather five-year journal that I love to write in at the end of the work day. For some reason, I like to write my books in September, and that's when I'm writing this book. So, I'm going to write in my five-year journal how many words I contributed to this book on this day. And next year, if I'm doing a writing retreat at the same time, I can see how I'm comparing, and see what I'm writing about next year. It's actually pretty fun.

The important thing is don't make it a huge thing when it doesn't need to be a huge thing!

What's the smallest thing you can do to apply the learning, then assess whether it was worth it? Pretty simple.

One of our challenges as leaders is to seek to get community buy-in when we want to do something. For major changes, that's important.

You know what gets buy-in: Results!

If you start doing something, and it works, people want to join in. Stephen MR Covey says, "Bottom line, whether you're dealing with restoring trust or establishing it in the first place, it is results that will convert the cynics."

Let's take a big educational issue that you can implement in small chunks. Garett Cook (episode 453) has been working with me for the past couple years in the mastermind, and he's done some amazing things with his staff. One of the things he has wanted to do is implement professional learning communities (PLCs) in his school. But he couldn't pull the trigger because it seemed like another initiative. Also, his teachers also believed they were implementing PLCs, even though they weren't. He took a different route. He saw the power in PLCs but instead of overwhelming he applied his learning in a simple way: he started talking to his teachers about their data. Not in an overbearing way, but just asking the four questions of a PLC, what do we want kids to know, how will we know if they are learning it, what will we do if they aren't (or are) learning it?

Then, he assessed whether or not it was working. Were his teachers engaging in this practice with him, or shying away from it? They were engaging, so they developed a way to implement PLCs that worked for his school.

You can do this for your school as well. Implement the smallest possible change you can make, and then dive in when people start asking for it.

This is how my podcast came to be. We did a school visit to an amazing school. I asked the principal if I could interview her further, and publish it on the internet. She said I could, and then I just kept asking people if I could learn from them.

From each podcast interview, I tried to implement something new, in a small way. It works really well.

When I read books, I do the same thing.

Be patient with yourself and your team as you try to improve your mind.

Body

We often overcomplicate physical health, when there is an easier way to deal with it.

My goal in this book is to help you be a transformative principal in simple, clear ways.

I'm certainly not an expert on our bodies, and I wouldn't try to be, but I have learned a few simple things.

As I mentioned before, be wise about what you put into your body and exercise.

Honestly, we could stop the chapter there and let you do your thing, but I do want to highlight something that I learned from Trish Wilkinson.

We can't separate our body from our spirit or from our mind. One without the others is incomplete.

Trish Wilkinson is the author of the book *Brain Stages* and was a guest on episode 443. She suggests two simple things to take care of our bodies every day, and as a bonus, they also help us get ready for tackling whatever we need to tackle each day.

1. Drink a tall glass of water in the morning.
2. Get 10 minutes of exercise.

Pretty simple, right?

Trish says, "I usually would get these really high scores and people would just be like, 'Wow, you must be amazing!' And I would just laugh because I know it had more to do with my kids getting a big drink of water and exercise" each morning.

Cell division, which is what makes our brains store long term memory, is encouraged by brief exercise and water, Trish teaches. And while most people think they don't have time for that, you do. And it is worth the effort.

Kelly Tenkely (episode 248) goes on a walk every morning with her school, students and staff. They walk for about a mile. She says it is to build community, but it also helps students prepare for the day and be ready to learn.

Your body is unique and different. Find some help to take care of your body in a way that works for you.

I hereby grant you permission to stop fad diets, stop trying to lose weight, stop trying to get fit.

Start by loving your body and all its imperfections. Love it for what it can do. Develop a mindset of love for your body. Respect it, and once you start doing that, you'll find that it is actually amazing.

I wish I could remember where I first heard this, but I've heard it dozens of time since. People who have tried to lose weight and get fit for years finally gave up trying to force their body to do something, and once they accepted their body for what it was, miraculous things started happening. Once they stopped trying so hard to lose weight, the weight started to melt away.

Taking care of your body is more about loving it as it is than it is about working out every day.

My advice is not to change, but to accept. Once you've accepted it, you may want to change, or maybe not. But if you don't accept it first, no amount of change will ever be long-lasting or effective.

Spirit

Your mind and body need their inputs and outputs. And so does your spirit. When we talk about spirit, we're not talking about religion. We are talking about the relationship between you and a higher power, or you and a higher purpose in your life. It could even be about your mindset. You can define it however you want, but my comments here will be tended more toward the spiritual, as in high power. I'm a Christian, and as such, my life and experiences are shaped strongly by that. I echo what a leader of my church once said in regards to people of other beliefs and faiths, "Let me say that we appreciate the truth in all churches and the good which they do. We say to the people, in effect, you bring with you all the good that you have, and then let us see if we can add to it. That is the spirit of this work." (meeting, Nairobi, Kenya, 17 Feb. 1998). I encourage and support you in defining your spirituality however you see fit, but above all else, define it! Then share it! Appropriately, of course.

Luke Foster wrote "A perennial worry about democracy: it produces unteachable, flat souls. Plato had described the situation in a democratic city as one of intellectual anarchy. No moral education is possible because egalitarians do not see any legitimate ranking among their desires" (2020).

This quote above demonstrates why we need to have spirituality, or some purpose to guide us. In my belief system, I believe that every child is a child of God, with limitless potential. That is not an idle thought or something that is just a nice thing to have. It drives me to make learning a positive and powerful experience for kids. It makes me want to do as much as I possibly can to help them reach their potential, whatever it is. Why?

"Once the [spirit] awakens, the search begins and you can never go back. From then on, you are inflamed with a special longing that will never again let you linger in the lowlands of complacency and partial fulfillment. The eternal makes you urgent. You are loath to let compromise or the threat of danger hold you back from striving toward the summit of fulfillment." —John O'Donohue (Gottfredsen, 2020).

Because my spirit has awoken, as John O'Donohue says. My spirit is awake, and I cannot help but do what it beckons me to do. I can't help but believe in kids, because that is so deeply engrained in who I am, I cannot deny it.

Certainly, our spiritual journeys are ours alone, but we do experience them with others, usually our family.

This is highlight by Jessica Cabeen from a special episode where I asked principals what they wished they knew when they started: "If I could go back to myself as a first year principal, I would say, take care of yourself. The job will always be there, but it's so critically important for you to take care of yourself and your family." Our family is connected to us in a different way than others. They are part of our spirit. Whether that's your family by choice or by birth, your family means something different to you than all the other people in your life. My spiritual belief is that our family relationships can continue beyond this earthly life. And to me, that means that when we finish our mortal sojourn, and we can still be around those that we love, we're going to want those relationships to be as strong as possible.

As Jessica says, the job of a principal is a full time job. It's always there, and there is always some fire that we need to put out. It's just part of the job!

Share Your Spirituality

When your spirit is awakened, share that with others. Help others see how important it is to you. This doesn't mean to preach, because it's not about religion, as I said before. It's about sharing your values, which we will talk more about in the vital vision chapter. It's about sharing what makes you tick. Here's another quote from Melissa Bernstein, "I think the cry of my own [spirit] to be seen authentically had grown so loud that I couldn't deny it any longer. You know, I wouldn't have come out with it if I had been so impelled to just finally say, I'm done hiding in the shadows, I'm done wearing a facade. I'm done denying exactly who I am and all my hypersensitivities and I just need to be accepted as who I am, because then perhaps I can help others be accepted as who they are."

Sharing your spiritual growth is an important part of what you do. But you can't cast pearls before swine and so you should ensure that the way you share and what you share is appropriate and meaningful for your audience.

Chapter Summary

Your self care is the tiny domino that starts everything else off right. You should take care of yourself because you are a human that deserves to be taken care of! No other reason is as important as that.

Your self-care is like a stool with three legs, mind, body, spirit. Taking care in each area prevents the stool from toppling over to disastrous effect in your life!

Accept yourself as you are before you try to change.

Inputs: What you put into your mind, body, and spirit makes a difference. Be wise about what you ingest in each of these areas.

Outputs/Exercise: Your mind, body, and spirit need exercise. Define what works for you and stick with it!

Key Questions

1. How does what you put into your mind, body, and spirit impact you on a daily basis?
2. What exercises are you currently doing to strengthen your mind, body, and spirit?

3. Are you getting enough sleep?
4. Do you have a hobby outside of work?
5. What's the one thing that you can start doing today to improve your self-care?

References

Covey, S. M.R. (2006). The SPEED of Trust: The One Thing that Changes Everything (p. 117). Free Press. Kindle Edition.

Foster, L. (2020). Tocqueville on the Mixed Blessing of Liberal Learning: Higher Education as Subversive Antidote. 10.1007/978-3-030-34937-0_4.

Gottfredson, R. (2020). Success Mindsets (p. 3). Morgan James Publishing. Kindle Edition.

Hinckley, G. B. (1998). meeting, Nairobi, Kenya, 17 Feb. 1998. https://www.churchofjesuschrist.org/study/ensign/1998/08/excerpts-from-recent-addresses-of-president-gordon-b-hinckley?lang=eng

CHAPTER TWO
Get Support and Give Support

Never tell people how to do things. Tell them what to do and they will surprise you with their ingenuity.

General George Patton

Example is not the main thing in influencing others; it is the only thing.

Albert Schweitzer

To go fast, go alone. To go far, go together.

African proverb

Talent wins games, but teamwork and intelligence wins championships.

Michael Jordan

Chapter Takeaway: Transformative principals get support for themselves, and give their teachers great support using whatever means work best in their situation.

This chapter is broken into two parts, getting support for yourself and giving support to others. First, we'll talk about support for yourself. Then, we'll talk about support for others. I combine them in a single chapter because they are both connected and many aspects bleed over. It's impossible, however, to support your staff if you're not getting support for yourself. This is one of area of the domino principle that really matters. If you took my advice in the beginning of this book and are taking care of yourself, it's going to be a lot easier to take care of others. Transformative principals take care of themselves.

My friend Danny Bauer (episode 448) uses a great model to describe great support. He's talking about professional development, but I think that it applies to support as well. He said, "A is for authenticity, B is belonging, C is challenge. And when you have those components integrated into a PD experience, it leads to life and leadership transformation"

When we are supporting our teachers, we need to be authentic, to help them feel like they belong, and to challenge them.

Authentic means that we need to address issues as they arise and not be silly about why they matter. Be focused and clear about what the problems are.

Helping them feel like they *belong* is powerful, and it lets them know that we want them here with us. We're authentic because we want them there. We're not being harsh because we want to get rid of them. We are authentic because they belong with us.

Finally, *challenging* means that we give them what they need, even when it is hard. We also know that we grow through challenges.

And here's the thing, you need the support for yourself as well. That's why I created the Mastermind, the best leadership development for school leaders, to give other principals the support that I know we need. It's also why I created a companion course to this book, called *How to be a Transformative Principal*. You can access the course at jethrojones. com/how2be.

Most of us love going to conferences and experiencing the infusion of great ideas. But most of us don't do a lot with what we learn there. It's like a microwave meal. It's passable and gives decent enough nourishment. But it's just not as good as a slow-cooked meal (crockpot or smoker, your choice). That slow-cooked meal makes the food melt in your mouth and is just delicious.

In the Transformative Principal Masterminds that I run, we have found this perfect balance of authenticity, belonging, and challenging. Each group has it's own name that evolves naturally. Ayisha (one of our members) got the idea for the name from her secretary, who said, "every time Ayisha left that meeting she acted more inspired." Ayisha left each of these meetings feeling and acting more inspired because she was getting the ABCs of support that Danny talked about.

They help you find success. They help you successfully support your teachers.

Let's start by talking about getting support for yourself.

Get Support

You Can Support Yourself

In a Mastermind meeting recently, Nick Gilles, a principal in Wisconsin, made a profound statement.

He was in his first year in a new building with a whole new office staff as well. He was clearly overwhelmed and was struggling to find the time and energy and information to accomplish all his tasks. He was in sticky-note mode, where he was trying to just get rid of all the sticky notes that had accumulated on his desk. While discussing with the group, we reminded him of many things that he could do and that he had done at his previous school to deal with all these unknowns.

It wasn't that Nick wasn't smart or didn't know how to do his job, but he was experiencing some challenges that prevented him from seeing what he had done. At the end of the meeting, he summed it up perfectly. He said that he was grateful we reminded him of things he had already done to be successful.

He said, "Sometimes you get so buried in your own wave, you forget the life preservers you've used before."

Wow. Insightful. Sometimes we do get buried in our own waves and we forget all the things that we have done to help ourselves get out of that situation. Growing up in Southern California and spending a lot of time at the beach, this analogy resonated with me. You can support yourself by thinking about your experiences that led you to where you are. You've got the experience, expertise, capability, and everything else you need to be successful, already within you.

Whether it is you or your teachers who need support, you each have the answers within you. Sometimes, it is really helpful to have someone pull it out from you. Sometimes, it is not that easy. Sometimes, you need a lot more help than you may even be willing to admit to needing, but it is possible to get to those answers.

What I want you to take away from this is that you can do it. Whatever it is. You can do it. And you can do it better with support.

Where to Get Support

There are several ways to get support for yourself. Of all the ways you can get it, I'm going to divide them up into three categories: crowd-sourced, expert-sourced, professionally-sourced. There's a big circle around the Venn diagram below because you are responsible for yourself, no matter what.

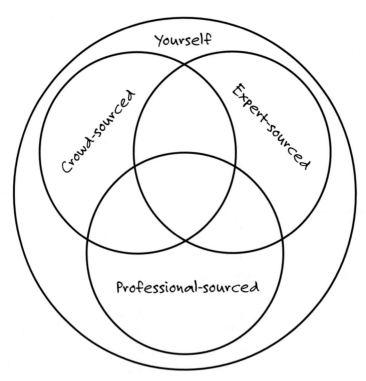

Crowd-sourced refers to anything that comes from the masses. There is typically no, or a small cost. Nothing is tailored for you specifically, though you can find some great support. Think professional learning networks, books, podcasts.

Expert-sourced refers to something that you pay more for because an expert has produced it. This is different from books because although an expert has produced a book, it is written for the masses, not for you specifically. Expert-sourced support is typically more tailored to you. Think courses, conferences, workshops, etc.

Professionally-sourced refers to getting help from someone who either provides the support professionally, as in that is their job or maybe they have a license specific to that support. The financial and time investment often go up here, although when a service is done for you, the time investment is quite minimal, but the financial investment is much higher. Think one-to-one coaching, masterminds, hiring a presenter.

Let's illustrate this with an analogy. Let's say something in your house broke, like a ceiling fan in the bathroom. You have three ways of getting support:

Crowd-sourced: Look up a video some random guy made that shows how to replace the fan. Your investment: a few minutes searching and watching, and however long it takes you to replace it yourself.

Expert-sourced: Your friend does a lot of remodeling of homes and he sends his worker to replace it for you or guides you through it. Your investment: You buy him dinner for his troubles or buy him a new tool that will be helpful for him.

Professional-sourced: You hire someone to replace it for you. Could be a local handyman or a licensed electrician. Your investment: Financial so you don't have to worry about it.

Each of these sources have their place for you at different times in your life. Don't discount something because it is free. And don't think something is exactly what you need because it costs a lot of money.

To put this in a more personal setting, I'd like to share a personal story. It's actually my wife's story, but it beautifully illustrates how this circle works. Several years ago, shortly after our last child, Eloise, was born, my wife's mom died suddenly. Nobody was prepared for it and it was very hard.

My wife sought support from friends, neighbors and people from church (crowd-sourced). It helped, and was fine. Or at least it appeared fine.

As you probably know, grief and loss can manifest in different ways, and it took 5 years for it to really manifest for my wife. She was really struggling and after a deep discussion, she went to see a therapist, who was licensed to help her deal with the grief of losing a parent (professional-sourced). She saw the counselor for about 6 sessions, and that helped. It was expensive financially, but worth every penny for her peace of mind and for overcoming the grief she was experiencing.

After those six sessions, she didn't really feel like she needed any more counseling, but knew that she needed something. She turned to a life coach to help her deal with the feelings of loss and deal with the expectations she still felt from her mom (expert-sourced). She chose a life coach because it made sense to her. She's been with that life coach for over a year now and has made tremendous growth in her mindset, ability, and capability to deal with emotions related to her mom. This costs money, but it doesn't break the bank, and the value is so high that it is easy to justify each month.

Different seasons call for different measures and the story of my wife illustrates how she dealt with something over the course of a decade.

Depending on your own situation, resources (not just money), experience, and attitude, you should seek different types of sourced support for yourself.

I strive to offer something at each of these three levels:

Crowd-sourced: My books (SchoolX, and this book, so far) and my podcast, Transformative Principal, with over 500 episodes, completely free, completely accessible to anyone. Investment is time to make yourself better.

Expert-sourced: My course that accompanies this book, How to Be a Transformative Principal (see more at https://jethrojones.com/how2be). My courses on Trauma. Investment: the cost of the courses and the time to learn the material shared.

Professional-Sourced: My specialized district trainings and Transformative Principal Mastermind. This is where I spend the majority of my time and effort preparing and supporting principals. See more at https://transformativeprincipal.com. Investment: Cost of membership and time each week to spend getting better with help.

In each of these examples, we go through the three different ways to get support.

Financial investment	Crowd-sourced	Expert-sourced	Professional-sourced
Time investment	Minimal	Medium	Done-for-you: low Done-with-you: high
Commitment	Low	Medium	High
Value	Varies	High	High
Support	Low/nonexistent	Varies	High

While it is easy to think we should get professional-sourced support for everything, I'm going to argue that that's not necessary.

What is necessary is getting the best help for you when you need it.

In my wife's example, we both agree that she would have benefited much more had she sought out counseling earlier. She might have even been able to avoid counseling altogether if she would have started life coaching earlier, even before her mother died.

We can't change the past though, so we need to think of our current situation and what kind of support we actually need to get through it. It will vary for each person.

Things we don't talk about: Principals who face discipline, investigations or suspension

There are some things we don't talk about in education—anything revolving around adults and discipline, investigations, or suspensions. These are really scary situations, and professionally embarrassing, so it makes sense that we don't talk about them much.

If you're facing this yourself, you can call me and I can talk you through it. I'm not a lawyer, nor a rep, but I am someone who cares about you and I know how alone you must feel right now. My phone number is (801) 7-JETHRO (seriously, that's (801) 753-6754, thanks Google Voice for letting me get my name in my number).

Dave Ramsey said that divorce is when a marriage turns into a business transaction. A work relationship is already a business transaction, but it doesn't always feel that way. There are a few things to remember if you ever find yourself in this unenviable situation.

Document Everything

Whether you're investigating or being investigated, you need to follow this rule. Document everything that happens. No matter how small or insignificant it seems. Establish a system and keep to that system. If you are being investigated, do not keep your documentation on your work computer. If you are investigating, do not keep the documentation anywhere but on your work computer!

Depersonalize

If you're an educator, it's already personal. But you have to take the personal sting out of it. Rick Jetter and Rebecca Coda were on the Transformative Principal podcast to talk about this (episodes 194 and 195). There is some reason that the other people have these feelings of ego, fear, jealousy, and so forth.

Rebecca said, "They may be getting pushed on from top down. It didn't start personal with you, but because of their own struggles, it [may have] become personal...It is the hardest thing to do [to depersonalize] if it does feel personal."

But you have to depersonalize it. This is especially challenging when it seems the accusations are unfounded.

The risk to not depersonalizing is that you will be too caught up in it and make it about you and how you feel, and you'll likely say or do things that you wouldn't want to.

Develop Relationships

This step starts way before anything bad ever happens. I had an information technology (IT) director who said to my face, "I didn't approve your order for technology because I don't like you." What? That's not a reason to not approve a purchase! Despite my best efforts, this IT director did not like me. I certainly couldn't control that, but I was able to go to the superintendent, with whom I did have a good relationship, and explain the situation. Sure enough, the technology got ordered, but

I can only imagine what hoops I would have had to jump through if the superintendent didn't understand where I was coming from and didn't have a good relationship with me.

Rick talks about needing to align yourself with others because often you need to find others who can be allied with you. He said, "If you're a lone soldier on a battlefield, you're going to die. But if you have an army behind you, you've got a chance to win."

Sometimes, it is all about who is having the conversation. Someone else may be more eloquent than you on a particular topic. And you may be that person for someone else. So be prepared.

When this happens, you need professional support.

Give Support

The Model

Rita Pierson (2013) said in her famous TED Talk: "Every child needs a champion." This is true beyond just kids. Every adult in your school needs a champion, too.

My niece, who was in high school at the time, bought a used Lexus SUV. It was in great condition but was several years old. I leaned in and looked at the odometer. It had just crossed 300,000 miles. That car had seen a lot. It had a single purpose the entire time. Its purpose was to get the driver from point A to point B day in and day out. For more than 300,000 miles. An engine requires gas, but it is not there to serve itself. It is there to serve others. I think that we as principals are similar. Our role is to serve others. Our role is to help people day in and day out. For years. We can be that engine for our staff and our students.

My educational philosophy is very simple: We give people what they need when they need it. This applies to support as well.

How Do I Grow Leaders?

One of the most important questions we can ask is "How can I grow leaders?" Why is this important? Because if your focus is on growing leaders, then it changes how you interact with your staff and students. If your purpose to mold people into perfect representations of you, you're going to miss out on the important growth and development their own strengths, abilities, and personalities give them.

It's a lot easier simply to train people to be like us. In fact, that's how our educational institutions have been for at least a hundred years. The purpose of making them "college and career ready" is actually a very narrow focus, as attested by our standardized tests, college entrance requirements, and grading systems.

This is not the section to talk about how wrong those practices are. We're going to shift this conversation to focus on the individual. Let's take an example of a student named Michelle, who is given the autonomy to find the best way to do the things she needs to accomplish. When you, as her principal, give her the space to be herself and develop her talents to be the best version of herself, you enable her to achieve something that you could have never dreamed of. You help her become a leader.

Let's talk about leadership. What is leadership? Patrick Lencioni said the "point of leadership is to mobilize people around what is most important." (p. 143) Imagine if you can find a way to help Michelle develop that skill. Now, imagine if you have a school of people mobilizing others around what is most important. Imagine how quickly assessments, grades, and the ennui of our current iteration of school would fade quickly into the background.

There are several other ways to define leadership, but I like this definition by Lencioni the best. Because it doesn't talk about making people do something. It doesn't talk about enforcing rules or expectations. It talks about mobilizing others around what is most important. If you're providing support to teachers and students and helping them be leaders, you're going to help them mobilize others around what is most important.

Focus On Them

Several years ago, Amy Fast (episode 133), a principal in McMinnville, Oregon, said something profound to me. I didn't understand it fully at the time, but I've repeated it to hundreds of people at this point. We were discussing how to support people and she was disgruntled by the fact that many people say we should fill people's cups so they have the energy to help others. She says, "In fact, I would even say when it is 'fill their cups as a means to an end.' Let's not fill their cups so that they can give to students but let's fill their cups because they're human beings and they deserve it."

Let's serve our teachers because they are human beings and they deserve that by virtue of the fact that they are human beings. As humans, we are too often transactional. We try to see what the benefit is for us if we do something a certain way. We try to find the justification for doing something when we often don't need to do that. We just need to do the right thing.

Transformative principals are not transactional, they seek to transform others into the best version of themselves.

As a leader in a school, we are surrounded by people we can serve. We need to remember that we are not in a job for our own benefit.

Greg Gardner, episode 431, a principal in Georgia, describes it this way: "I look for problems that could arise for my teachers, and then I focus on eliminating those problems from ever being an issue for them." Greg takes his approach of helping his teachers very seriously. All through the pandemic, he worked to solve the problems that existed before they had a chance to distract his teachers.

Support doesn't always mean what you think it means

Support doesn't always mean what you think it means. When we think of support, we often think that it means we are going to stand behind our teachers and support (where they mean *affirm* or *endorse*) their decisions.

I've always told my teachers that I'll support them, but I won't endorse their bad decisions. We must move away from the idea that support means agreement. Support means that we help them get better. Sometimes, we do that through difficult conversations and high expectations. Sometimes, we just get them support from somewhere else. Other times, it means we stand by them and affirm or endorse whatever decision they made.

Geoff Woods (episode 1045) talks about how to support someone when they are struggling. He shared an example of someone who wanted to get to a better position. He modeled the type of conversation to have, and this included calling out the bad behavior as a way to support that person. He says, "I know that ultimately, one day you want to be [achieve this goal]. Which way do you think gets you there by being the type of person who points the finger or by being the type of person who first and foremost asks, what can I do differently, and then comes up with a solution and executes that way?"

Supporting someone often means that we bring accountability. Geoff says, "Bringing accountability to the table in those conversations is actually something that's helping them advance in their career. See the difference? Accountability does not have to be this tough word. It doesn't have to have a negative connotation. It can be as simple as, "Hey, I hear that you're saying this."

In our conversation, the topic was around a teacher that was controlling students. How do we support teachers who are controlling students?

Geoff continues, "You're not a puppeteer. You can't control them. [Ask the teacher] 'What can you do differently to help that student take a stand for that student's greatness instead of allowing them to fight for their limitations?' Now, did that sound like I was laying down the hammer? No, no, not at all, but I'm reinforcing that we don't think that way. And if it continues, that's when the heat can ratchet up."

You may need to increase the pressure as a way to support a teacher. You may need to even fire a teacher as a way to support her. One of my teachers was just amazing. She was so inspiring and good at what she did. But she was having struggles at home and while it wasn't impacting her work, yet, it likely would have in the near future. We both understood she couldn't keep going at work, but neither of us wanted her to leave. Supporting her meant giving her permission to take care of her family issues. It meant letting her leave our school, where she made a huge impact and made it better for everyone. It wasn't firing her, but rather giving her permission to put her family first. It was actually a lot harder to support her by letting her stop teaching than it was to fire other people.

Bryan Hyosaka (episode 428) is a teacher at an innovative school in Denver that is located in a bike shop and a coffee shop, by design. He talks about support with the students: "I don't think that, hearing that you weren't as successful as you want it to be is the news you want to hear, but I think at the same point, if you're giving the feedback all along the way, and if you are having open and honest conversations with students along the way, then there's also not this grand surprise. You know, for us it wasn't as if, out of nowhere, they're like, 'Oh, what happened?' I meet with every student individually once per week. We're constantly conferencing. We're constantly role-playing and strategizing together. And so I think, first of all, there wasn't a surprise for them. But there was a sense for them of 'I understand what went wrong. I understand what role I played in it, and I understand what I can do better next time.'"

While Bryan is talking about students here, the same applies to teachers. If you're not giving support in a positive way, but rather bringing accountability and consequences to them, it shouldn't be a surprise. We need to be communicating early and often about the challenges their facing.

Chapter Summary

We all need support. Find the support that is right for you right now. Change when it is no longer the right kind of support. Provide that support for your teachers.

Sometimes, we need aggressive support that reminds us what we are capable of and how we can be our best.

There are three kinds of support: crowd-sourced, expert-sourced, and professional-sourced.

Ultimately, you alone are responsible for all your problems. That's empowering.

Key Questions

1. Do you have the support you need right now?
2. What kind of support do you need? Crowd-sourced, expert-sourced, professional-sourced?
3. What kind of support do your teachers need?
4. Do you have a plan of support for each teacher?
5. Are you meeting regularly with your teachers to provide support?

References

Clear, J. (2018). Atomic habits: An easy & proven way to build good habits & break bad ones. Avery.

Lencioni, P. (2012). *The Advantage: Why Organizational Health Trumps Everything Else in Business.* 1st ed. Jossey-Bass.

CHAPTER THREE
Strengths & Delegation

Never doubt that a small group of thoughtful, committed citizens can change the world. Indeed, it is the only thing that ever has.

Margaret Mead

Management is doing things right; leadership is doing the right things.

Peter F. Drucker

Lead and inspire people. Don't try to manage and manipulate people. Inventories can be managed but people must be lead.

Ross Perot

As we look ahead into the next century, leaders will be those who empower others.

Bill Gates

The great accomplishments of man have resulted from the transmission of ideas of enthusiasm.

Thomas Watson

Delegation Is About People
Chapter Takeaway: Transformative principals know that delegation is more about people than it is about tasks.

Now that you're taking care of yourself and getting support, you're probably realizing that things are starting to fall off your plate. You might be missing some things in the name of self-care, and that doesn't feel good. You probably are starting to feel like you're letting people down or not doing your job well enough. Now, what we need to think about is how to delegate properly.

I hate to start a chapter out this way, but I've got to say it. You've thought about delegation wrong your whole career.

You see, when we think about delegation, we think about tasks. What we really need to think about are the people to whom we are delegating.

The recurring theme in this book is that leadership is *people* more than anything. That applies to delegation as well. If you start with people, your results are going to always be better.

Let's take a crazy example. Why don't accountants advertise how many audits the Internal Revenue Service (IRS) conducts on their clients each year? Imagine for a minute this ad, "JJ Financial: Over 500 audits conducted by the IRS on our clients!"

I don't think that would get many clients walking through the door. When you're delegating your taxes to someone, you're not going to delegate to someone who regularly does it poorly enough to get audited by the IRS.

Here's another example. If you want your first-born, your pride and joy, to be a basketball star, are you going to go find a basketball coach or are you going to find a Sherpa?

Although these examples may sound crazy, let's bring it home. Are you going to delegate taking care of kids who get hurt in an elementary school to a hospice nurse who hates kids? I sure hope not.

Here's a real-life example from my school. Laura Thurneau was a seasoned administrative assistant in my district, and she applied to the school I was just named principal of. Wow! Lucky me. Hiring her was an easy right choice. She excelled in the interviews and did an amazing job. She excelled at everything. But, sure enough, a couple days into the new school year, an angry parent called. Laura was the sweetest woman you'd ever meet, but she didn't like getting yelled at. She told me there was an angry parent on the phone and she had been pretty rude when Laura was trying to help her.

I told Laura that we don't tolerate that behavior from parents, students, teachers, or anyone. That's not how we deal with issues. I delegated the authority to hang up on someone to Laura. I directed her to do that and said it was a requirement from me. When they called back, she could hang up on them. Let me state that as clearly as I stated it to her. I directed her, "When an angry parent calls and starts yelling at you for something someone else did, you need to hang up on them. If they call back, let me answer the phone."

Guess what Laura didn't do? Laura didn't hang up on anyone! Laura could not imagine hanging up on someone. I had delegated a task to her that she would never be able to accomplish. It was absolutely the wrong thing to do. The direction was clear. The task was clear. The ask was simple. Hang up on rude people. Don't take their anger yourself.

A couple of angry calls later, when she still wasn't doing what I asked her to do, I understood a different way to get the result I desired (that Laura wouldn't get yelled at by angry parents). I delegated a task that Laura was really good at. I told her to transfer people to me directly (even to my cell phone if I wasn't in the building). She was really good at helping people and getting them to the right people. Sure enough, as soon as someone was rude to her, she said, "Let me get Mr. Jones." Then, I could have the difficult conversation with the parent.

That enabled me to start the conversation with the parent like this:

"Hi, Mrs. Smith, thanks for calling. Before we get to the thing you called for, Laura just let me know that you're pretty hot under the collar. I'm happy to help you, but I can't have you calling and giving the staff here grief. They can't do anything to help you when that's how you're acting. Now, I'm happy to help you, but we aren't going to have a heated conversation. What's on your mind?"

Asking Laura to participate in a confrontation with a parent was the wrong thing to do.

Here's another example. During the pandemic hybrid teaching mess we all endured in one way or another, Margaret, who was head of school in an international school in the United Arab Emirates was working hard to schedule kids as they were coming and going, which still happened even though there was a pandemic. The scheduling became complex, and she learned quickly that using the new scheduling software they adopted over that summer was going to be challenging for her new assistant principal (AP).

Back up a couple months. Margaret knew that she couldn't be in the weeds as much as she was. She was really excited about her new AP but knew that he still had a lot to learn. She knew she needed to delegate to him, and she was starting to do that.

Margaret was frustrated that she was doing all the scheduling and knew she shouldn't be the one doing it. When she sat down with her AP to teach him how to do it, she realized that she was the best person for the job. She didn't want to be. This task was the AP's. But as she realized how much knowledge she had to transfer and how little time she had, she realized that it wasn't the right thing to do to delegate this task to him even though it should have been his.

In a different time, with a normal schedule, this would have led to a different outcome. She looked at the situation, determined who was best suited for the task at hand, and recognized that it was really her. She was frustrated by this, but knowing that the best person was working on it helped her feel much more comfortable with the plan. Recognizing she still needed something off her plate, she found other tasks that her AP and others were better suited for, and she was able to do the scheduling work herself.

She looked at the situation, and even though the task should have been the AP's, she knew she was the better person for it. So she didn't delegate that. She delegated other things that were better suited for him specifically.

Contrast that story with another situation where a middle school principal did the schedule because he liked it. After he retired and the new principal came in and expected the counselor to schedule students, the counselor was incredulous because that was "the principal's job!" Well, the new principal wasn't the best person for the job. The counselor was. The old principal also wasn't the best person for the job but he just really liked it, so he did it. Many other tasks that the principal should have been working on didn't get accomplished because he was too busy doing something that he should have delegated.

Here's the challenge you are going to face. You'll likely believe more often than you should that you can just do it better, faster, and easier than anyone else. For the first half of the year, Margaret just assumed she could do the scheduling better, faster, and easier than anyone else. It wasn't until she looked at all the knowledge that she kept in her head (and not documented!) that she realized she had painted herself into a corner where she really was the best person for the job. She started putting processes into place so that she would be able to confidently share that burden with someone else who could be trained appropriately and take that off her plate.

Look at the matrix below to see how to make these decisions about delegation. And pay close attention to the person, not just the task:

Your Skills			Other Person's skills		
Not app			Not app		
Bad	Good	Great	Bad	Good	Great
Delegate ASAP	Delegate Soon	Don't Delegate	Don't Delegate	Start Delegating	Delegate ASAP

Your skills

Not applicable/Bad	Good	Great
Delegate ASAP	Delegate soon	Do yourself

Others' skills

Bad	Good	Great
Delegate ASAP	Delegate soon	Do yourself

This brings up a few questions that we'll tackle here:

What if you really are the best one to do this? Are you really the best? Does this task help you achieve your goals and vision for your school? If so, then yes, you should be doing it. If no, then you need to delegate or stop doing it.

How do you delegate in stages as others are learning?

What if they need support and training but you don't have the budget/time/resources for it?

What if nobody has great skills? What if we are all bad (especially with a new program)? You have to find a way to get that training, because that is what someone really needs.

As you are going down this path of delegation, you have to recognize that every minute anyone is working in their weakness is a waste of their time. You have to know your people well enough to make sure that they are living up to their potential and using their strengths as much as possible.

Sometimes, as the leader of a school, you have to do the awful work. Sometimes, you have to contact trace, even if you are really awful at it. But just because you have to do it now, doesn't mean you have to do it forever! You've got to get yourself out of the skills that you aren't great at.

In one of my schools, I wrote the newsletter every week, and it took me forever. When I started working with Laura, and my AP, Dr. Courtney Orr, those two were much better suited for that task and performed it flawlessly, and quicker than I ever could.

In episode 76 with Will Parker, he talks about delegating effectively. And encourages us to give instruction on the front end to make sure our expectations are clear and more effective.

Will utilizes what are called KRAs, or Key Responsibility Areas, which help people know exactly what in their responsibility. KRAs are very simple, and succinctly list out what areas a person has full responsibility over.

A couple good examples of what could be on an Assistant Principal's KRA:

- First responder to discipline situations for last names beginning with A-L

- Full formal observation protocol for the following teachers…
- Safety practices (contact tracing, mask enforcement, fire drills, active shooter training, parent pick up & drop off, etc.)
- Lunch supervision

These areas of responsibility then become the areas where the AP has first say in how they come about.

Michael Hyatt recommends a strategy for keeping track of what level you are comfortable delegating to people.

> *Level 1: Do as I say. This means to do exactly what I have asked you to do. Don't deviate from my instructions. I have already researched the options and determined what I want you to do.*
>
> *Level 2: Research and report. This means to research the topic, gather information, and report what you discover. We will discuss it, and then I will make the decision and tell you what I want you to do.*
>
> *Level 3: Research and recommend. This means to research the topic, outline the options, and bring your best recommendation. Give me the pros and cons of each option, then tell me what you think we should do. If I agree with your decision, I will authorize you to move forward.*
>
> *Level 4: Decide and inform. This means to make a decision and then tell me what you did. I trust you to do the research, make the best decision you can, and then keep me in the loop. I don't want to be surprised by someone else.*
>
> *Level 5: Act independently. This means to make whatever decision you think is best. No need to report back. I trust you completely. I know you will follow through. You have my full support.*

KRA's fall in the Level 5 delegation. You may not be able to delegate to people at Level 5 to start out.

In episode 192, Naphtali Hoff helps us recognize that we can delegate management activities. Leadership belongs to everyone, but management can be delegated.

We all struggle with delegation, but we have to remember that we delegate the most important work in schools every single day: teaching. If we can delegate that, certainly we can delegate so much more.

If you've done the work on getting to know your people and their strengths, delegation will be much easier.

Too often in schools, we think we have to be a hero to everyone by doing everything. We feel like we sometimes have to be the martyr that dies so other people can live. This is not a healthy way to be a hero.

Being a Hero

So what is a hero? And how do we become a hero in the right way? *Who Not How* (2021) is a book by Dan Sullivan and Dr. Benjamin Hardy. Well, kind of. Actually, not a word of it is written by Dan Sullivan. But the ideas are his. Benjamin Hardy just used his skill as an author to write the book that Dan didn't really want to write but that needed to be written. "*Who Not How* is truly that simple. You define the vision, find the Who or Whos, and let them create the result." (p. 10) As I mentioned previously, delegation is about people, not tasks. Find the right person for the job.

Dan understands the power of delegation, and the whole book is clear evidence of effective delegation. Dan delegated the book to Ben. And when Ben asked Dan what advice he had for writing the book, Dan was nearly incredulous. He said, "Why would I tell you how to write this book? You're the one who writes these types of books. I wouldn't even begin to know how to advise you on this, nor would I want to." (p. 19)

Too much in schools, we try to focus on the *how* rather than trusting our people to do what they need to do because we have explained the vision clearly enough. One page 140 of that book, Dan (via Ben) states that the leader needs to be a hero for their team. That comment ruffled some feathers in my principal masterminds. We talked about this at length and nearly every principal said they didn't feel comfortable being the hero or calling themselves the hero. What Ben is really saying, though, is that the leader needs to be the *who* for the people in his organization as well.

One of the principals I work with saw very quickly when he went to a new school that there were certain people who jumped at the opportunity to help and improve things, and others who didn't want to do anything extra and always asked for what they would get in return. This of course leads to the 80/20 rule, which states that 80 percent of the work is done by 20 percent of the people. This harsh truth leads to burnout in that 20 percent. They see themselves pulling a tremendous amount of weight and others seemingly coasting along. For the 20 percent, the principal can be a hero by removing as much from their plate as possible. For the 80 percent, the principal can be a hero by finding something that will engage that person's strengths, abilities, passion, time, and energy. Sometimes, of course, you can't always find that.

Another principal, Eric, was inspired by our conversation to ask his teachers, "What would it take for me to be your hero?" This is not a question that principals would typically ask. This is a question that almost seems uncomfortable to ask. Should we really even be striving to be someone's hero? Is that what we are here for? But think about it a little deeper. What do you need to do for your staff for them to say, "I love working here, and it's a joy to go work for someone I see as my hero!"? Most principals I know are service oriented, which is heroic, but they think being a hero is a pedestal they shouldn't be on!

You may be thinking that you don't have enough time to be someone's hero. You don't have enough time to ask everyone what you need to do to be a hero and then do that stuff because you have a mountain of other work to do already! This is a valid concern, but it's transactional. Transformative principals think longer term than their to do list.

There is a multiplying factor when delegation happens effectively and when people play to their strengths.

I was fortunate enough to have a leader who was a hero to me when I was a young man. Because I saw him as my hero, I was willing to do things that were difficult for me. I was willing to be my best even when I didn't believe that I deserved it or was good enough. That's what a hero brings out in you.

If you are delegating effectively and finding ways to support others, I believe that you can be a hero to them.

One last story to illustrate this. When I lived in Russia, a bunch of the other missionaries I was serving with were musically gifted. In fact, I was the only one who wasn't. My 10th grade choir teacher asked me to mouth the words.

When this group wanted to put on a concert, I was supportive, but immediately felt left out, because I believed I couldn't sing well and add my support. What I am great at is being a cheerleader, so they asked me to be the conductor and master of ceremonies. They were all musically gifted and didn't need me as the conductor, but they did want my energy in front of them and to get the crowd excited about our songs.

Because they delegated this responsibility to me, they gave me an area to contribute in a circumstance where I was truly the weakest link. They were my heroes for including me, when they didn't have to. I was their hero because I could use my strengths to support them!

This beautiful relationship turned into a powerful lesson for me that has stayed with me all this time.

Strengths

The lesson I learned from conducting music was that I did have strengths, but they weren't performative. Knowing your strengths doesn't mean that you are arrogant or prideful. Knowing your strengths means you know what you are good at, and you should clearly, humbly, and honestly express that. These other people were good at singing. They weren't demeaning to me because I wasn't, but they encouraged me to accept that I was good in front of a crowd, and one of the better Russian-speakers that wasn't actually Russian. I could actually tell jokes in Russian, and when you can tell jokes and make people laugh in a second language, that is real skill. That's what we needed for that concert.

So, how do you even learn your strengths? Well, here's the thing about strengths. We all have them. Thanks to the internet, there are all kinds of personality tests out there you can take to help you gain more insight into yourself and what you think and value.

I do trainings with leadership teams using personality profiles, and I always give this disclaimer. Whatever you are using, it's a framework to help you get out of your own head and think in a different way. It's not the be-all-and-end-all! It doesn't define you, you define the personality test!

I can't stress this enough, because if something doesn't fit with what you want to believe about yourself, just ditch it. Why? Because being beholden to some test someone else devised doesn't define you.

But, when you can use it as a framework to help you learn and grow and become better, you can find a lot to like about it.

Another benefit of most personality profiles out there is that they pretty much all value whatever it is that you are doing. Most personality profiles don't say, "You are X and X is bad!!!" Wouldn't that be silly? Yes, you do have weaknesses, but there is probably someone else who has a strength in that area.

I want to remind you of the special ed teacher I hired who was bad at paperwork and scheduling meetings. In our school, we didn't need her to be good at those tasks because we had a Who for that! It's certainly okay to find the right person for the job.

For leadership teams, and for most education situations, I find the DiSC personality profile (Personality Profile Solutions, 2021) to be my favorite. The DiSC addresses conflict and communication. I have found that poor communication and poor handling of conflict are two of the most common underlying problems that lead to things not going well in schools.

My suggestion is to find a personality test, take it, and then see how it can help you. If you want my help in doing that, just reach out and I'll help you.

Connie Hamilton (episode 191) spoke about looking for strengths of teachers by conducting walkthroughs. The walkthroughs are completed and then analyzed for shared strengths throughout the building. The added benefit of this approach is that you can find the needs and the instructors for this professional development the same way. Connie said, "As a collective leadership team we analyze that information that we have collected in the observations, looking for patterns of strengths and maybe some next steps for professional learning for the building as well. And then those recommendations are shared with administration and they make the fall plan for your school."

Jim Knight (episode 417) is perhaps the most knowledgeable person in the world when it comes to coaching teachers. He also recommends starting with strengths. We talked about the challenges of setting professional development and goals around things that some teachers are already proficient at. Jim said, "That's going to be the issue with any goal.

You're going to have some people who have knocked it out of the park and some people who are just beginning and those people who have got transition time that's less than 5 percent would be working on a different kind of goal. This is complex work. If what you're doing is working, keep doing it, whatever it might be. But my general sense would be you need to have transparent and honest conversations about what's happening. You need to face reality."

Sometimes, that reality is that teachers don't have enough strengths yet to be ready for something that you're pushing on them. At times, that means that there are enough who are already at that level that you don't need to make it a schoolwide focus, but really just something that you have to do to lift the bottom percentage up to a higher level.

Again, though, you need to focus on strengths. You can't force people to do things, and you must invite them. Jim continued, "I don't see myself as trying to get teachers to do something. I see myself as creating a context where teachers can flourish. And that means I'm not trying to persuade them really of anything. What I'm trying to do is put systems in place so they can excel. And that's why coaching is so important, because the coach meets with each teacher, talks to them like a professional, and helps them set a powerful goal that will make an unmistakable positive impact on their lives."

Although they can't always see that the approach will make an unmistakable positive impact on their lives, it's still a valid goal to try to attain. Jim stated, "I'm not trying to do a number on them or get them to do something. Motivational interviewing is a whole approach to therapy that says much the same thing. That resistance really isn't the issue. The issue is a misalignment." And when there is misalignment, and we're talking about strengths here, they may not see their strength or weakness in a given area.

Jim continued, "Assuming they're professional, then, I really want them to have a meaningful say in what they do. Otherwise, they're not going to be that committed to it." And this is key, not only with adults but with students as well. If they don't see the value in what we are proposing, they're not going to be committed enough to do it. This is an important reason why we start with strengths. It's a lot easier for people to see that it's possible to get better in areas of strength than it is to get better in areas of weaknesses. Our weaknesses are often screaming at us all the time. It's much easier to say, "This part I'm actually good at, and I wonder if I can get even better at it!"

Using CliftonStrengths (formerly StrengthsFinder; https://www.gallup.com/cliftonstrengths/en/strengthsfinder.aspx) can help you know what you are good at if you don't already know.

Thom Markham, the "father of project-based learning," pleads for every teacher to take a personality profile to learn about their strengths and weaknesses.

The book *Strengths Based Leadership* by Tom Rath (2008) is a seminar on this approach, and although it was not written for education specifically, it does provide great insight that educators will find helpful.

Chapter Summary

Delegation is about people, not tasks. Figure out what you're bad at, and delegate it. Figure out what you're great at, and do that. Allow others in your building to do the same.

Figure out *who* is the best person and leave the *how* up to them.

Do the work to learn the strengths of those you work with, share with them what they need to be successful, and help them in areas they are weak.

Key Questions

1. What am I great at? (The list is not as long as you think!)
2. What am I not great at? (This list is probably longer than you'd like to admit!)
3. Am I delegating tasks to the right people? How can I know?
4. Do I know the strengths of my teachers?
5. How can I learn their strengths better?

References

Hyatt, M. (2019). *The Easier Way to Delegate for Perfect Results.* https://michaelhyatt.com/the-five-levels-of-delegation/

Personality Profile Solutions. (2021). *DiSC personal assessment tool.* John Wiley.

Rath, T. (2008). Strengths based leadership: Great leaders, teams, and why people follow. Gallup Press.

Sullivan, D., & Hardy, B. (2021). *Who not how: The formula to achieve bigger goals through accelerating teamwork.* Hay House Business.

CHAPTER FOUR
Vital Vision

Vision without action is a daydream. Action with without vision is a nightmare.

Japanese proverb

The vision is obvious to the leader, because they know it, and so they assume everyone else knows it too—but how could others know it unless the leader shares the full picture?
Michael Hyatt, The Vision Driven Leader (2020)

Your values are only worth what you're willing to pay for them!
Richard Shell

Chapter Takeaway: Transformative principals know that without a clear vision, nothing else you do will matter. Transformative principals take the time to create their Vital Vision.

A compass doesn't tell you when you are wrong, but if you check in with it, you can find the right path again. A compass seeks to get you back on course. That's the same role as a vision in a school. It's not like a GPS, which will reroute you to get you to your destination. But if you check in with it, it will tell you if you're going in the right direction; if the vision is clear enough, it will help you know what you should be doing to get it right.

Purpose, Mission, Vision, Values

This section about vision is really going to talk about all aspects that go into the vision: purpose, mission, vision, values. We throw these terms around, and not everyone is consistent in explaining what they are. I want to make sure it's clear what we are saying because it can get a little confusing. And, this is honestly one of the biggest problems with mission and vision statements: Nobody knows what they really mean!

Really, you have to define each of these things specifically for your school, and it's not enough to just adopt what the district has to offer. Bob Sonju talked about the relationship between them in episode 31: "Once you come to consensus on a purpose, then you're able to begin to describe the vision of a perfect school. I've often described this as just your school's vision and what you want to become, what your target is, in order to accomplish your purpose."

Clearly, our purpose is to educate kids, right? Yes, but that's not enough. Bob said that there are three things you need to do: "First is purpose, something that compels you to action. Second is describing that perfect school or your vision, and then three, what are we going to collectively do to make sure that we meet those things?"

In our discussion, Vital Vision is the combination of having *purpose, vision, mission, values,* and *norms.* You have a Vital Vision when you have all the elements in place. If you're going to do purpose or values, you might as well do the rest, because they are all interrelated.

Purpose: *Why am I here?* The thing that pushes you to action. Educating every child is cliché, and probably doesn't push you to action.

Vision: *What's my view of what this would be like if everything were perfect?* A vision is aspirational. If you ever arrive at your vision, it's time to upgrade it to the next level.

Mission: *What specifically am I going to accomplish?* This is the day-to-day actions that you need to do to accomplish your vision.

Values: *How will I make decisions to get to my perfect school?* These are the beliefs that make it possible for you to achieve your perfect school because they inform how you act when you have difficult decisions to make.

Norms: *How do we behave?* These are the actual behaviors that you believe will get you to your perfect school.

Quick explanation of how this works. I worked with Damon Hargraves at Kodiak Middle School. We had a vision of where we wanted the school to go. Damon described it as that mountain peak, over there (vision). We both wanted to be at that peak, so we worked every day to get there (mission). If we made it to the peak, we would find joy and happiness (purpose). We could choose how to get to that peak that worked best for us (values). And finally, we would check in occasionally to make sure we both still on the right path (norms).

Purpose *Why am I here?*

A purpose needs to compel you to action.

In order to understand your purpose, Mary McMahon, at the time president of the Alaska Association of School Principals, suggested asking these questions: "What does the school of your dreams look like? Are you currently leading the school of your dreams? And what are the behaviors of the staff? What matters most to you when it comes to educating our children? And why did you choose this profession? Why did you choose to become a principal or educational leader?" (episode 128)

Both she and Bob articulated that it's about knowing what the school of your dreams looks like.

If your purpose is to prepare kids for next year, you'll never live up to your potential. Your purpose has to be bigger than that. As a child, I was a bit of a punk. I would get under my teachers' skin just for the fun of it. None of them would believe that I'm actually writing my second book about school leadership! Oh, if they could see me now! Many teachers threatened me that my behavior was going to get me in trouble. Here's how it went.

In lower elementary: "Jethro, you may think this is funny now, but when you get to upper [grades 4, 5, 6] elementary, they're not going to let you get away with this behavior."

In upper elementary: "Jethro, you may think this behavior is OK, but when you get to middle school, it's going to have to stop. They're not going to tolerate it, and you're not going to like it."

In middle school: "Jethro, we're trying to prepare you for high school, and you're just not getting it. This behavior won't fly in high school. They will give you Fs. And may suspend you, too."

In high school: "Jethro, you may get away with this here, but in college, if you even get in to college, they won't be as lenient as I am. I'm trying to prepare you for college."

In college: "Jethro, I don't know why you even showed up today. No matter how well you do on your final exam, you won't pass this class. You might as well not even be here. And if you act like this in your job, you're probably going to be fired. I'm just trying to prepare you for the real world."

In my job: "Jethro, you can't play sound effects from a soundboard app on your iPad during our meetings." "Is that because you don't like it, or other people don't like it, boss?" "Other people don't like it." "That's not what I hear. After every meeting, they tell me they think it's hilarious and helps them get through the boring meeting." "Well, it's not appropriate, and if you think you're ever going to be a principal with that kind of behavior in meetings, you've got another thing coming!"

I heard these things my whole life, and then became a teacher and heard all my peers saying them. Then I became an administrator and heard other administrators say them, although I knew from experience that it was a bunch of baloney. Everybody puts up with what they get. They like to project a future where someone is going to finally have enough and say something. Well, it doesn't usually happen. All this to say that if we are blaming our own inadequacies on some future consequence for a student, no student will ever care about what we are doing.

Do you want to know what finally changed my behavior? A perceptive teacher asked, "Jethro, how does it make you feel when you act this negative way versus this positive way? I've seen you act in both ways. Which one makes you feel better and more true to who you are?" That teacher had a purpose. Her purpose was to help each one of her students grow up to be the best that they could be. That day, it was specifically me. That experience has stayed with me because it forced me to confront the reason I was misbehaving all the time. It also helped me know what kind of person I wanted to be. By that simple act of questioning, without judgment, she helped me see that I had potential far beyond what I was currently living up to. Now, did that make me perfect? Obviously not. But she was the only teacher I had who was preparing me for more than my next stage.

Is your purpose strong enough to compel you to have that kind of a conversation with that punk kid? Your purpose compels you to take the necessary steps to do what needs to be done.

Vision *What's my view of what this would be like if everything were perfect?*

Once you have a purpose, you can start to paint a picture of you living up to your purpose every single day, and everyone else in the building doing the same. It's helpful to ask, if this school were perfect, what would it look like?

In episode 129, Scott Beebe talked about sharing a vision story rather than a vision statement. A vision story is more powerful because it paints the picture better than a vision statement. Stories are how we as human beings have communicated for thousands of years. In our conversation, Scott asked me to describe where we could go on a trip to illustrate a vision statement. I told him we're heading to Kodiak, Alaska. Scott explained, "All you've told me is a vision statement. We're going to Kodiak. That's where. That's the destination. Because that's what vision is. It's the ultimate destination of where you see your [school] going in the X number of years. That's the vision statement, but I've got nothing else to work from. So, I kind of fill in the vacuum with my own concepts. So, if a school comes up with the vision statement that 'we want to create great kids,' you know, just in its simplest form, we see great kids. Okay. What constitutes a great kid? What does a great kid look like? What sort of things might it take to get to a great kid?"

After this conversation, Scott asked me to describe Kodiak and what we would do if he were to come visit me there. I described how it is an adventure! You can talk about how the journey here is a story in and of itself because we live on an island. When you think about Kodiak itself, what's it going to be like when you're here? It's beautiful, with the sun shining for 13 hours during the day. If you come a little bit later in the summer, you're going to have the sun all day long and you'll find that the sun energizes you and makes you have energy to stay out so that you'll be out doing something outside and it'll be 11 o'clock at night and you'll be hungry. And you won't understand why, because you've got so much energy and you're not tired yet. You're going to be engaged in fun activities like fishing, ATV, hiking, and camping, you can do all those things here. And then if you're really lucky, you're going to get to see a Kodiak bear, which is the biggest land bear in the world. The only one that's bigger is the polar bear.

With that kind of vision story, you get a much better idea of what the future can hold. Let's relate this to our schools. If we define the vision for our school as "we produce great kids!" then it's not only pretty vague, but it's something that likely everyone wants to aspire to. Instead, let's paint a vision story of a school that creates great kids. Here's an example of the school I ran during the pandemic:

> *Imagine having a student who drives their own learning.*
> *Imagine having your student's gifts and talents highlighted in their schooling, no matter what those gifts and talents are.*
> *Imagine having a school experience that is tailored around your student and your family.*
> *SDL Academy is the personalized solution for your child's education. We focus on and highlight your child's strengths and use them as the basis for instruction.*
> *Students are given real-world problems to tackle, while teachers follow behind and ensure that the standards kids should be learning are being measured and assessed.*

This vision story gives you an idea of whether you want to be involved in this school or not. It invites those to whom it calls to be part of it. It repels those who don't catch the vision!

If you have a vision story, it's easy to see if you fit there or not. Scott said, "It is okay for people to say no, that's not really my bag. In fact, it helps you. Because the people you want to lead are people who want to go where you're wanting to take the ship. The problem is most leaders don't know ultimately where they're taking the ship."

Regardless of whether your school district has a vision, you must have one for your school. It can (and should be) close to your district vision, but when people decide to enroll (the Seth Godin version of enroll) in your school, they will want to know if they are going to experience the same things that you want to experience.

Here are a couple of weak vision statements that don't produce any kind of idea of why I would want to be there:

"A community united to improve the quality of life through education." (Independence [MO] School District, https://www.isdschools.org/vision-statement/)

"The El Paso Independent School District will be a premier educational institution, source of pride and innovation, and the cornerstone of emerging economic opportunities producing a twenty-first century workforce" (https://tx02201707.schoolwires.net/site/Default. aspx?PageID=886). This is a little better, but what does it even mean? The purpose of school is to create a workforce? The purpose of school is labor? Is that what we really want?

"Vision: Every graduate ready for college, career, and life." The training Boone County School had for vision statements before coming up with this vision statement emphasized succinctness.

The following are all from a website (HelpfulProfessor.com) that is supposedly helping people write vision and mission statements. The problem here is that you can't just adopt what other people have written. Your vision story has to be for your people. "We foster our students' love for learning, encourage them to try new and exciting things, and give them a solid foundation to build on."

"Our vision is to develop well rounded, confident and responsible individuals who aspire to achieve their full potential. We will do this by providing a welcoming, happy, safe, and supportive learning environment in which everyone is equal and all achievements are celebrated."

"We believe that a happy child is a successful one. We are committed to providing a positive, safe and stimulating environment for children to learn, where all are valued. We intend that all children should enjoy their learning, achieve their potential and become independent life-long learners."

"Our early learning center exists to provide a safe, developmentally, inclusive environment for toddlers, preschool, kindergarten and school age children."

Here's a better vision statement from the School District of Palm Beach County (https://www.palmbeachschools.org/about_us/district_mission_and_vision_statements):

We envision...
The School District of Palm Beach County is an educational and working environment, where both students and staff are unimpeded by bias or discrimination. Individuals of all backgrounds and experiences are embraced, affirmed, and inspired. Each and every one will succeed and flourish.
The School District of Palm Beach County will take ownership for students' academic mastery, emotional intelligence, and social-emotional needs by creating environments where students, families, staff, and communities will develop agency and voice.
A joy of learning is fostered in each student and a positive vision for their future is nurtured. Each student's cultural heritage is valued and their physical, emotional, academic, and social needs are met.
...WE SEE YOU.

You want your vision story (or statement) to attract people who want to be part of the organization you are creating.

Let's look at the Vision for the Greater Dayton School (episode 391):

From the very start we were determined to look at education differently—that includes our definition of success. So while the federal government, state government, school districts and individual schools focus on test scores and other measures of academic achievement, we focused instead on the only metric that matters: what kinds of people our school produces.
Our school will start with preschoolers. But our strategy started by envisioning our alums as 27-year-olds. At that age, we have a pretty good indication of what kind of people they're going to be long-term. (In fact, brain science tells us the frontal lobe isn't fully developed until the age of 27.)
And at that age we'll conduct the final round of data-collecting in a longitudinal study that will track our students' progress. So, what do we hope our 27-year-olds will be? Our goal is that at least 80 percent of them are ...

- *Successful by their own definition*
- *Physically and mentally healthy*
- *Living lives of character and integrity*
- *Financially independent*
- *Established in a career*

Once we determined the finish line, we set out creating research-based mile markers—starting with 4-year-olds—that will ultimately create the intended outcomes and ultimately pull families out of generational poverty.

If you're not interested in helping kids all the way up until (and probably beyond) their age of 27, you're probably not going to be interested in working at this school. Hiring is the most important thing you do, and you can determine if someone is a good fit pretty quickly.

Scott Beebe describes how powerful vision is:

When you're hiring people right now, you're kind of hiring on a whim and I don't mean that as any offense at all. It's just true because you're hiring people, and frankly, they don't know where they're going, because usually you don't know where you're going or at least you haven't articulated that.

Vision is not a novel thing. This isn't something that Harvard business review just kind of concocted a couple of decades ago. Vision is age old in fact, depending on your theological bent. For me, I'm very much of the thought that God created this world. And in that creation, he had to have vision because there, there was nothing but expanse before this. And so, he had this vision created this world, and now you get to live on a beautiful island off the coast of Alaska. I get to live in shore from a beautiful island off the coast of South Carolina. And God dreamed this whole thing. And so, there was a vision at the outset, and then it goes through all of this Jewish ancestry where God gave vision to these different people. We even have an entire nation state today. The nation of Israel that came out of a vision that was given to Abraham thousands of years ago. That's how powerful vision is.

If your school is just another school, you can't have a vision that will compel people to join you, unless you want people who are just looking for a job, any job, and as soon as they find a better job, they'll leave. This will also attract families that just want babysitting for their kids: "Any school will do as long as they keep the kids there all day and don't send them home!"

Mission Statement *What specifically am I going to accomplish?*

Having a vision for your school enables you to attract people to do what? Scott Beebe explained that a mission statement is different from the vision story. It's like a summary of the vision story. It's the work you do. He said, "This needs to be meaningful. People need to be able to bite into this and get substance out of it. And so basically once you've got your vision story written, now, what I usually have people do is go through their vision story and highlight key adjectives, key action statements, words, phrasiology in there." Then use that to make the mission statement. So, if motivation is a key feature of the vision story, then motivate would be a key word in the mission statement. He said, "If the vision is the destination, your mission statement is the vehicle you're going to drive to get there." He also said that mission statements should be memorizable. So the vision story is a story that you can tell in several different ways in several

Your mission statement should also match your culture. For example, if you are in an area with lots of rivers, lakes, and streams, then it would probably make sense to use a phrase like, "We help kids navigate the world around them" as a way to signify that our specific community understands that navigate means something special to us. If you're in an area with lots of farmland, bring that imagery and culture into your vision story and mission statement. If your in an urban environment, bring that imagery and language in as well.

Nobody wants to be "just another school." But that's what you are when you have neither a clear mission statement nor a clear vision.

Scott offered one other piece of advice that I think is really important to our conversation, and other guests on the podcast have disagreed with Scott on this: "I would not bring other people into the vision, by the way. It's got to be the leader's vision, but the mission, you can start to bring other people in to get their insight and keywords." A vision is also different from a mission statement in that it isn't a collective, wordsmithed vision written by committee to appease everyone. A leader has to have a clear vision of the school. It's just a necessity. That's your role as the leader: to define the vision for the school. Then get other people to help make it happen.

Here are a few mission statements (again from helpfulprofessor.com) that get to the daily work that you do:

"Our mission is to provide high quality education in a safe, respectful and inclusive environment that builds a foundation for life-long learning."

The doing work is high quality education, safe, respectful, inclusive. The foundation for life-long learning hearkens back to a vision statement.

"Our goal is to build skills that set children up for success in kindergarten and beyond."

The doing work from this mission statement is building skills for kindergarten.

"Our mission is to provide a safe haven where everyone is valued and respected. All staff members, in partnership with parents and families are fully committed to students' college and career readiness. Students are empowered to meet current and future challenges to develop social awareness, civic responsibility, and personal growth."

The doing work from this statement talks about a safe haven, focus on college and career readiness, empowerment, social awareness, civic responsibility, and personal growth.

These were just examples to illustrate the point. I have no connection with Butte School District, but I just stumbled upon their web site that lists their vision, mission, values. It can be found on their web site at https://www.bsd1.org/about/mission-statement/. Their mission statement is as follows:

"Butte Public Schools will create, in partnership with our staff, families and community, challenging opportunities for all students to be successful as they become responsible and contributing citizens, and master the knowledge and skills essential for life-long learning in our changing and diverse world."

The daily work words they are using are challenging opportunities, contributing, mastering knowledge and skills.

And one more example, since Palm Beach County's vision story was so good, here's their mission statement:

"The mission of the School District of Palm Beach County is to educate, affirm, and inspire each student in an equity-embedded school system."

They daily work words are educate, affirm, inspire, and equity-embedded.

The final thing to ask about a mission statement is: does it accurately describe what you do?

Palm Beach County is going to be very hypocritical if they are not equity-embedded. That means every day they are working on equity. They've taken the right next step to define equity: "Equity means each student—regardless of race, ethnicity, poverty, disability, language status, undocumented status, religious affiliation, gender identity, and sexual orientation—will have access to the opportunities, resources, and support they need to imagine, nurture, and achieve their dreams."

Core Values *How will I make decisions to get to my perfect school?*

In order for your daily actions to manifest, you need to know how to act when you have a difficult decision to make. Your core values help you make those decisions. Again, everyone has their own core values, but it is so valuable to share these with your staff and community so everyone knows what we believe and what matters most.

G. Richard Shell (episode 449) says that your values are only worth what you're willing to pay for them. He wrote a book called *The Conscience Code* to help people know how to make decisions. It's a powerful take on the importance of core values.

Mary McMahon has been teaching principals about establishing and sharing their own core values for years. She does this with her staff every year. She said, "What I do at the start of every year is I share the top 10 things that matter most to me on the very first day with my staff. As a leader, I can't emphasize enough how important it is to do that, to be very clear about who you are as a leader, and Todd [Whitaker] would concur. In *What Great Principals Do Differently* (2020), he said that great principals establish clear expectations at the start of the year and follow them consistently as the year progresses. And so, my question for all school leaders and principals is 'what matters most to you?' And whatever that answer is, when you really identify what matters most to you needs to be shared with your staff so they understand who you are and where you're coming from."

Mary reads this list to her teachers each year and invites them to do the same. She also recalibrates to make sure these are the ten things that really matter to her.

Your core values are the beliefs that make you tick, and not just as an individual, as Mary shared, but also as a school.

Shell says there are three types of values: "Career success in any line of work depends on taking responsibility for three things: doing things right (duty-of-care values), doing the right thing (ethical values), and being the right kind of person (character values)." (G. Richard Shell, *The Conscience Code: Lead with Your Values. Advance Your Career.*)

Each of these three types of values should be part of the values for our schools. Again, when everyone knows what they are, they will invite the right people to work with us and enroll in our school. When they are, people want to be there.

I want to highlight the beliefs and values from Butte School District No. 1 and identify the type of value of each:

- A safe and caring environment will exist in all schools. (Duty-of-care)
- Education will be a primary responsibility and investment of society. (Ethical)
- Butte School District No. 1 staff members are valued. Staff members will be involved in professional growth and development activities. (Duty-of-care)
- Students' self-esteem is important; they will feel valued as human beings and successful as learners. (Character)
- All students will learn to become responsible partners in their education and contributing members of their community. (Duty-of-care)
- Students will develop a foundation of technological knowledge that will enable them to access, use and evaluate information. (Duty-of-care)

- Cultural and social diversity are strengths—feelings and beliefs of others will be respected. (Character)

By having these values, the school district is helping people identify how they will make decisions.

Shell also states that "When you face a difficult values conflict, systematically consider four factors: Consequences, Loyalties, Identity, and Principles." (G. Richard Shell, *The Conscience Code: Lead with Your Values. Advance Your Career.*)

This CLIP acronym helps you know when your values are being violated, and how to make the right choice, even when it is challenging.

So, how do you define your values? Well, you can start with how Mary McMahon suggests by just stating what matters most to you. As an example, I believe that all kids can learn, and my value is that all kids can learn from each other, so when I make decisions about learning environments for my students, it's going to include that value and it's going to be easy for me to lean towards inclusive environments over segregated environments. It makes it easy for me to decide that we are going to do coteaching instead of pullout special education.

Norms *How will we behave?*

If the values are what we believe, then the norms are the behaviors that exhibit those values. Pedro Noguera (episode 213) said that one of the best ways to build culture is to be clear about what norms exist in the school. He said, "It's about the norms that are present within a school. It's about the way people are treated every day. And as leaders, principals play a major role in shaping that culture. And you do that by developing a vision and sharing that vision with your staff and getting their input into that vision. And from there developing a plan to start to create a place that affirms the importance of children and their education."

The norms are how we behave day in and day out. Amy McDonald, who trains students and adults on being inclusive and supportive shared how norms are important in our school communities in episode 229. She's talking about webs of support for students. She said, "And social norms we talk about as that wind that goes through your web and positive social norms can lift your web up and help keep that balloon buoyant. On top of the web, a negative social norm can be that wind that pushes your web down. And in some areas of the world, those negative social norms are so strong that people choose not to live there. When we talk to teenagers about social norms, we validate the idea that changing negative social norms is really, really difficult, but amplifying positive social norms is a lot easier. So, we try to identify positive social norms that are happening in their schools and communities, and talk about ways that they can increase those positive social norms or add value to those positive social norms."

The norms that happen in your school are what you tolerate and value. Negative norms exist in schools, but we usually don't workshop those and publish them throughout the school!

My friend Eric Makelky is fond of saying your norms are whatever behaviors you're willing to walk by and not comment on. Powerful.

But they exist! In episode 143, Randy Sprick, of Safe and Civil Schools, reminded us that if doctors still need to be reminded to wash their hands, we can take a few minutes and remind school staff about appropriate social norms.

When norms are violated in our schools, it's incumbent on everyone—teachers, principals, students, noncertified staff—to address it. Randy gave a good example of how that conversation can go: "Randy, you are such a valued part of this staff. You are so important to the kids that you have in class. But I got another complaint, Randy, from a parent, who said that maybe you are trying to make a joke, but when you say that word, you're a fifth-grade teacher. Randy, when you say publicly to a kid, this work looks like a second grader. You may think you're making a joke, but that was hurtful. That child went home crying. Randy. I can't allow this in our building. Who we are as a staff is a staff that never belittles anyone. And I know that you're such a good teacher, Randy, that this may have just been you having a bad day. But if you don't work to rebuild that relationship with that student, I won't be able to support you with this behavior."

As a principal, you must establish norms that are appropriate for your building. What's the behavior that you're not willing to walk by without commenting on.

It's especially hard for teachers, staff, and students if they don't know these norms.

How do you create them?

First, you bring them up! That's such a simple step, but so many principals miss it! You've got to talk about it. And you've got to talk about it often!

When Vision Is Implemented Effectively

Vision is something you don't have to refer back to because it is who you are. I received this email from a Erika Johnson, a principal in Wisconsin. Her insight is powerful:

> Here is a copy of the vision statement we did for our Building Leadership Team. It's funny, as a team **we haven't looked at this in a very long time—we haven't had to**. It became what we believe in and we haven't had to refer back to it. If I remember correctly, I had discussions with certain staff I wanted on the team and shared what I wanted to move forward; once the team I wanted was assembled, we wrote the vision statement together and everyone signed it. From there, we did our norms and got to work. The best thing we did together, and one of the first things we did together, was to have kids submit ideas for a new school motto; we picked the top 8-10 (that aligned with our vision) and let kids vote on it. Our school motto is "Work Together...Win Together...Strengthen Our World." The second kids felt like they had a voice in our school, everything changed. Our students and staff truly believe in this and for the past 8 years it has become who we are. Interesting how it all comes together.
>
> Here was the Vision/Mission Statement we drafted almost 9 years ago:
>
> "Engage in authentic conversation centered on creating an atmosphere that breathes "Kids First," this is our core. As a building leadership team, we will identify areas of strength and be honest about areas that need change and act on them. Together,

we will move forward with identifying best teaching and learning practices. We will create genuine change that will be felt beyond the four walls we teach in."

Erika is a principal who knows what is important. She set a vision with her team several years ago, and they haven't had to refer back to it because they know who they are.

This may sound simplistic, but it is true. If you have to constantly remind your team "who we are," then who you are is not really ingrained in their minds.

You need to establish a vision for your school, regardless of where you want to go.

My friend Bridget Belcastro, a principal in Chicago, told me in 2018 about her process to teach her students about GRIT—Greatness Requires Internal Toughness, starting in 2015 (episode 260). It sounded pretty awesome. I talked to her three years later, in 2021, after the pandemic had rocked our world. She was telling me about her updated goals and how they wanted to be the best school in her county. I mentioned that being number one is about more than just test scores, but also it's about student success. She nonchalantly said, "Yeah, I think we have the mindset part down. Now it's about getting those test scores up."

She had worked diligently on creating things that would make success happen, shared her vision with her staff, and then they got to work. She didn't completely ignore test scores but knew that teaching GRIT was more important than just test scores. She was clear on her vision and her team knew it, and they knew how to implement it. Then, when they had implemented it, she knew the next steps that she needed to take involved getting those test scores to reflect what the kids were actually learning.

Sometimes, we think that we need to get new people because our current people aren't catching the vision. That's on us as leaders. Eric Chagala (episode 251) didn't hire any new staff to accomplish his vision:

I think one of the interesting things about our story is it's an actual true school transformation. I think sometimes a lot of people talk about school transformation, and then they talk about the new building they got, or I'm hiring a brand-new founding faculty or starting with a brand-new set of students. It's exciting for us because we had a group of students who were matriculating through and we kept them and the teachers who were at the old school that we transformed from stayed. All but one, and we were able to bring three new people on board. And so, you know, we did it with same kids, same teachers, same place.

And the way that we really worked around that was having a common vision for what our hopes and aspirations were for children. And then figuring out a way using the design thinking process to actually get there and what we discovered in using the design thinking process, that, that helped us gel together as a community.

Eric didn't allow the challenges of his veteran staff dissuade him from finding success in his new transformation. They completely redesigned their school, as he said, by "having a common vision" for the hopes and aspirations for their students.

The Leader's Role

How can you be a leader like Eric and get your entire staff on board with a new vision? In Who Not How, Dan Sullivan and Benjamin Hardy define leadership: "Creating and clarifying the vision (the 'what'), and giving that vision greater context and importance (the 'why') for all Whos involved. Once the 'what' and 'why' have clearly been established, the specified 'Who' or 'Whos' have all they need to go about executing the 'How.' All the leader needs to do at that point is support and encourage the Who(s) through the process" (2021, p. 10).

In The Advantage, Patrick Lencioni extends the responsibility of achieving that vision to the leadership team: "A leadership team is a small group of people who are collectively responsible for achieving a common objective for their organization" (2012, p. 21).

Regardless of how big your school or district is, you need a vision for your school. It is not enough to just tag along with whatever the other people are doing.

Tony Sinanis (episode 19) explained how the lack of vision in his district caused him problems at his school. He said that there were resignations and multiple superintendents in succeeding years and "the vision kept changing. There was no vision, so it was a challenge."

With all of these, you have to align to your district. If your district believes something completely different from you, or has a vision that is incompatible with your vision, you're not going to last long in that district, nor do you want to.

Chapter Summary

Purpose: *Why am I here?* The thing that pushes you to action. Educating every child is cliché, and probably doesn't push you to action.

Vision: *What's my view of what this would be like if everything were perfect?* A vision is aspirational. If you ever arrive at your vision, it's time to upgrade it to the next level.

Mission: *What specifically am I going to accomplish?* This is the day-to-day actions that you need to do to accomplish your vision.

Values: *How will I make decisions to get to my perfect school?* These are the beliefs that make it possible for you to achieve your perfect school because they inform how you act when you have difficult decisions to make.

Norms: *How do we behave?* These are the actual behaviors that you believe will get you to your perfect school.

A Vital Vision includes purpose, mission, values and norms.

Key Questions

1. Have I articulated what I believe about school and learning?
2. Has my staff had the opportunity to tell me what they believe about school and learning?
3. Does your vision align to your district's vision?
4. Do your values, mission, and norm align with your district?
5. Ask your teachers what they believe the vision and mission of your school are. If they can't articulate it, what can you do to help them understand it?

References

Hyatt, M. (2020). The vision driven leader: 10 questions to focus your efforts, energize your team, and scale your business. Baker Books.

Sullivan, D., & Hardy, B. (2021). Who not how: The formula to achieve bigger goals through accelerating teamwork. Hay House Business.

Whitaker, T. (2020). *What great principals do differently: Twenty things that matter* (3rd ed.). Routledge.

CHAPTER FIVE
Observations & Feedback

*It doesn't make sense to hire smart people and tell them what to do;
we hire smart people so they can tell us what to do.*

Steve Jobs

*Whether or not you can observe a thing depends upon the theory
you use. It is the theory which decides what can be observed.*

Albert Einstein

*A pile of rocks ceases to be a rock when somebody contemplates it
with the idea of a cathedral in mind.*

Antoine St. Exupery

*Chapter Takeaway: Transformative principals observe teachers and
students often to evaluate whether the vision is being implemented.*

Why do we do observations? Most of the time, the answer to this
question is for evaluation. In reality, the purpose of any observation in
our school is to see if our Vital Vision is being implemented. Once you
have a Vital Vision, your observations take on a different meaning. While
we usually talk about observations being related to classroom teachers,
this approach enables you to observe adherence to your Vital Vision
every day, in every thing you do. This certainly doesn't mean more
paperwork and more filling out forms, but gives you more information
about what is going on in your school.

If we don't have our vision outlined clearly and don't know what we
are looking for in our observations, we should not do them. Most of us

just do observations without putting much thought into it at all! It's just something that we have to do. Any training we receive in our district relates to how we should do observations as they relate to the evaluation process, not what is best for ourselves and our teachers.

Again, if you're not going to do observations intentionally, you should just not do them!

Before/Current	After
Transactional	Transformational
Feedback	Conversations
"Glows & Grows" (judgment)	Questions
Dissecting	Building
Evaluation	Adherence to vision

I made the table describing how my thoughts on observations have changed over the years. See the table that follows, and fill it out for yourself. What are your current thoughts and beliefs about observations? And what do you want them to be in the future?

Before, my thoughts about observations were that they were transactional. We needed to complete so many per day, week, month, and year, and we needed them for the purpose of evaluation. As I grew, I learned that my observations could become transformational.

In the beginning, it was about judgment and leaving feedback (positive or negative), and later it was about conversations and asking questions. It was silly for me to go to a teacher who had twice as much experience as I did and tell her what she was doing was wrong. When I started asking questions and having conversations, I learned that I didn't need to include judgments! She was usually very aware of her own shortcomings and could ask for help if she trusted I could actually help!

Before, it was about dissecting the lesson and picking apart all the things that could have been better or different. Later, I learned it could be about building a better learning experience for the students.

Finally, I learned what observations are really for. They're not for evaluations. They're for determining whether or not my vision for the school is being carried out. When I finally understood that observations tell me how well I explained the vision, it really changed everything. The focus went from, "You're doing this wrong (or right)" to "Perhaps I haven't done a good job articulating what school is supposed to look like!"

Transformative principals understand that the solutions to their challenges lie with them.

Walking out from each observation, I should be able to answer the question, "Have I explained my vision well enough to this teacher?" If the answer is yes, that's great. If the answer is no, I need to spend more time articulating it. Once I made that mental connection, I was able to say, "The problem is with me. I haven't done a good job explaining what I am looking for." Do you know how freeing that is? It's freeing because you can control you. You can't control anyone else, and it's marvelous to be able to control yourself and know what you need to do.

Before/Current	After

The Purpose of Observations

Many principals don't do many observations. In my first year of teaching, my principal came to my classroom to observe only for the required-for-evaluation purposes.

Too many jokes over the years have referred to administration as the "dark side" for a reason. Teachers feel like principals (or worse, coaches) are looking for what teachers are doing wrong, and that's not healthy for anyone.

If you're doing observations just because it is a required aspect of the evaluation, you have already lost the game. Transformative principals are more focused.

Teachers need support just like principals need support. Observations can be a key way to provide that support, if done properly.

Another problem we face in education is that we think observation just refers to observing the act of teaching. If our purpose is to evaluate teaching only, then yes, that makes sense. But that's not how transformative principals look at observations.

When we see observations as check-ins to see if the school vision and mission are being fulfilled, then we take a different approach.

One year, my assistant principal and I logged more than 1,200 observations in teachers' classrooms. We made it our mission to be there in their rooms on a regular basis. We learned so much from those seven observations per day. It was certainly worth it. Because of those observations, we knew for sure what was happening in our school. And it enabled us to make dramatic changes very quickly.

Even still, when our observations were focused on just evaluation, it wasn't helpful.

Transformation from Transactions

Where some teachers and principals see observations as a checklist, or transactional activity, transformative principals see them as a transformational activity. When observing a teacher (in their planning, teaching, collaborating, grading), we are looking to ensure that the school vision is being implemented, and where it's not, we seek to give guidance on how to make that work.

First, let's take a medical example.

In 2017, my daughter started complaining of knee pain. She has an incredibly high pain tolerance and for her to complain about something hurting was a big deal. We lived in Alaska at the time and didn't have access to the best medical care. She had an X-ray and it was clear. Then the doctor suggested we check the hip, and we saw that she had Legg-Calvé-Perthes disease, which is typically not a big deal. Most kids grow out of it and they can have normal lives.

Legg-Calvé-Perthes disease is where your femoral head dies and stops getting blood flow. It results in the breakdown of the hip ball joint. We took her to a specialist, and he said, "She'll grow out of it." And in the doctor's office, as I was asking more questions about the disease and how it affected kids with Down syndrome, he said to me, "I'm sorry, I've already spent so much time with you. I need to see my other patients. You can set up another appointment if you want to ask more questions." Keep in mind, we had to travel either by plane or make a seven-hour car drive to see this doctor.

To say I was frustrated would be an understatement. I use this analogy to point out that we are dealing with people in our profession. We are not dealing with widgets. The people we spend time with have feelings, emotions, worries, and cares. And ignoring or treating them as though they are a transaction is not a good way to deal with them.

Bringing this back to education for a moment, think about how your teacher would feel if you gave them some critical, possibly disturbing, information, and then said, "Sorry, I don't have time to deal with this, we've already taken too much time."

Of course, your teacher would be upset that you dropped a bomb and then skedaddled! My friend Damon calls this "seagull leadership"— swoop in, leave a mess, and then take off.

Being transactional is not helpful.

So, we took my daughter to a different specialist who had experience working with kids with Down syndrome. We asked him what he saw and what he expected for recovery. He said, "I've seen this in hundreds of kids with Down syndrome. We want her to have a full life, free of pain, where she is able to do the things she wants to do. I would have operated on this six months ago to ensure that we could stop the breakdown, because kids with Down syndrome react to this particular disease differently."

Rather than be annoyed that he spent so much time talking with me, he took the time to view our relationship as an opportunity to transform my daughter's life and make it better for her. By the time we were able to arrange surgery, as he predicted, her bone had started to heal and instead of being a round ball, now had a heart shaped head, with the sides of the heart growing part inside and outside of her hip socket. OUCH! In this case, it took several surgeries for the problem to be healed, and it's nowhere near where we want it yet, but we have much more confidence in the doctor who sees our relationship as a way to transform our daughter's life to be all she wants it to be, and not just as a transaction.

I share this story because we as principals in the name of "instructional leadership" go into conversations with teachers all the time with a transactional approach. We act like we know what is right because we are the instructional leader, and we expect them to do as we say.

I've been guilty of this myself. In one school, a longtime teacher did not do well according to our newly adopted evaluation protocol. She signed her final letter to the staff and me with her final rating on the evaluation. We had reduced her to her number, as we saw it. Embarrassing.

It doesn't have to be this way, and I vowed to myself that I would never treat a teacher like that again. She was right, and I was wrong. I had made her feel like she was just a number.

When I learned how to be a transformative principal in this regard, my goal wasn't to get teachers to teach in a specific way, it was to help them see the potential they had for being the best teacher they could. Teachers were willing and eager to respond to my feedback, questions, insights, and suggestions when I took a transformational approach.

Feedback or Conversations

Nobody likes being told they're doing something wrong. When people say they want feedback, what they really want is someone to say how great they are. Nobody wants to be told how to improve.

I'm reminded of an episode of the TV series *Ted Lasso*. A former captain, Roy Kent, of a football team is brought back as a coach. Kent hated his former teammate, Jamie Tartt, with whom he completely butted heads. Kent didn't want to give him any feedback. Tartt asked for help from the other coaches and Kent's girlfriend, Keeley. She suggested that Tartt do what she did, which is just agree with everything Kent said. So that's what Tartt did. Kent eventually agreed to give Tartt feedback. And he gave him some harsh feedback. Tartt did actually want some feedback but didn't like the feedback that he received.

It wasn't until it became a conversation that Tartt responded to the feedback. And this is what we need to learn about feedback. Feedback is one-directional. It goes from the principal to the teacher in an "I'm-in-charge-you-have-to-listen-to-me" kind of way. Feedback is almost always a complete waste of time.

The opposite of feedback is conversations. Conversations about instruction are different from feedback about instruction. When we're not doing conversations about instruction, we do silly things like "compliment sandwiches," where you put compliments on either side of critical feedback. Honestly, who doesn't see through that? You put time and effort into puffing up someone's ego just to tear it down and then puff them up some more. Ridiculous. And yet, there are people out there saying we should do just that!

I'm sure you've experienced some comment from someone about "being in the principal's office" and immediately feeling like they are in trouble. It's a thing. We know that. Making up a compliment sandwich to remove that feeling just doesn't work.

Instead, we need conversations about what we are seeing in teachers' classrooms and in their work.

In the book *Fierce Conversations* by Susan Scott (2002), she shared a story where she was hired to talk with an executive group about having fierce conversations. Mark, the leader, would not make eye contact with her while they were talking beforehand. She told him that this disturbed her and showed that he did not trust her, when they should be collaborating.

"Half an hour later as Mark introduced me, he said, 'Susan practices what she preaches. I know. She told me I had lousy eye contact and that it didn't feel very good. So I'm going to work on that'" (Scott, 2002, p. 119).

This example illustrates that powerful feedback, when given, makes an impact. But it doesn't happen as a blunt "You're doing this wrong." It's part of a conversation. That's what Susan had with Mark, a conversation about his lack of eye contact.

Susan went on to describe the kind of feedback she advocates we give and called it a conversation from the very beginning: "Fierce feedback is a conversation in which we have the opportunity to see what we may not see" (Scott, 2002, p. 158). Susan posited that feedback can be positive, negative, or neutral. She also goes on to define when we need to give feedback and when we need to have a confrontation. I talk more about this in the chapter on communication (chapter five).

Before having this conversation, Susan suggests that we take a very important step, and this applies to educators perhaps more than anyone else: "Before giving feedback, contemplate your reality. Is your interpretation what you saw or heard exact, or could there be a different interpretation?" She continues, "...we make up stories about people and then behave as if our stories are true" (2002, p. 163). Stephen MR Covey says in Speed of Trust that we evaluate others based on their behaviors and evaluate ourselves based on our intentions.

We need to stop giving feedback and simply start having conversations.

A New Definition of Instructional Leadership

In the book *Who Not How* (Sullivan & Hardy, 2021), Hardy explained how Sullivan reacted when Hardy asked him for feedback on writing the book. Sullivan said, "Why would I tell you how to write this book? You're the one who writes these types of books. I wouldn't even begin to know how to advise you on this, nor would I want to" (p. 19).

What if we used this approach for giving feedback to teachers? Would we be negligent in our instructional leadership?

Sullivan and Hardy define leadership differently. They say leadership is "creating and clarifying the vision (the 'what'), and giving that vision greater context and importance (the 'why') for all Whos involved. Once the 'what' and 'why' have clearly been established, the specified 'Who' or 'Whos' have all they need to go about executing the 'How.' All the leader needs to do at that point is support and encourage the Who(s) through the process" (Sullivan & Hardy, 2021, p. 10).

Let's think about that in terms of instructional leadership. As Justin Baeder defines it at principalcenter.com: "Instructional leadership is the practice of making and implementing operational and improvement decisions in the service of student learning."

I'll combine these two to define instructional leadership for transformative principals:

"Instructional leadership is the practice of establishing the vision for the school, defining why it is important, and supporting and encouraging teachers and students to make that vision a reality."

Too many programs have sought to make principals feel like they are the instructional leaders and so must have all the answers to all the problems that everyone faces. That is bad advice, and yet, that's what many principals feel they must do—have all the answers.

For example, in episode 89 of the *Transformative Principal* podcast, Dr. Robert Dillon encouraged listeners to be humble and not think they had all the answers. He said that it's important to have a bigger vision of how you're contributing to education as a whole beyond just the impact you're having on your school, but to be humble enough to recognize that no leader can have answers for everything.

Curiosity from "Glows and Grows"

After talking to principals about this idea of having conversations instead of just giving feedback, principals often assume that they should give only positive feedback. It's tempting to take the above advice to the next logical conclusion and commit to the following: "I'll just give positive feedback and only point out the good things that are happening."

Although that's certainly a positive intention, and one way to run your school, that's not what I'm talking about. Glows and grows is a strategy whereby a principal leaves a note with glows and grows (or has a conversation about it), and it is akin to the compliment sandwich. Principals sometimes feel a compulsion to "leave a comment about where a person can improve" as a way to ensure that they are not giving only positive feedback. Perhaps this stems from the fact that 97 percent of teachers are proficient in their evaluations (Colorado Department of Education, 2014).

Rather than focus on just giving feedback, take advantage of the fact that you aren't the teacher and be curious. Chris Horton said at the 2017 Transformative Leadership Summit: "Use curiosity about the situation and extend the conversation to where they want to go, not where you want to go" (Jones, 2017, http://transformativeleadershipsummit.com).

What does this look like? It looks like being curious about what a teacher did in their classroom. It is not interrogative but, rather, curious.

You observed a teacher and she asked students how they got their answer to a math problem. Several students described approaches to how they got their answer, and the teacher stopped after one different response was given.

As I share a glow, grow, and then express curiosity, think about which statements lead to conversations, and which are one-sided judgments.

Glow: Your strategy of showing different ways to achieve an answer was effective.

Grow: Give more students the opportunity to share how they got the answer or do a pair-share where they share with each other and then share their partner's response.

Curious conversation: I noticed you asked students how they got their answers. Five students gave the same response, and you moved on when the sixth student said they used a different path. Tell me about that.

Glows and grows are one-sided, they tell the teacher your judgment about something that happened. Curious conversations are you asking the teacher why and how she is successful (or not).

Having given hundreds of glows and grows in my career, I can clearly tell you that it was not very often where my glows or grows were unique or original to my teachers. In most cases, they had been doing this a lot longer than I had and they already knew what other options were out there. When I learned how to have a curious conversation, my teachers started reporting to me that I was actually helping them be better teachers.

Albert Einstein said, "I know quite certainly that I myself have no special talent. Curiosity, obsession and dogged endurance, combined with self-criticism, have brought me to my ideas."

Curiosity and self-criticism will help people know what they need to do better, faster, and more effectively than if we prescribe what they should do.

Building Instead of Dissecting

Ultimately, we want our teachers to be the best they possibly can be. There was a time in my career when I thought I needed to help people improve, and the way that I could do that best was by sharing my innate and amazing wisdom with anyone who would listen.

You can probably imagine how much my teachers liked hearing me spout my knowledge on a given topic, when they had so much on their plates already!

I was in a mode of dissecting what people around me did. It wasn't healthy or helpful. Everybody was waiting for me to come in and chop them down. I had no idea this was happening until someone used the above skills on me. People had given me feedback that I was intimidating and overzealous and that I acted like I had all the answers, but it wasn't until someone asked me how I thought people perceived me that I was able to see the error of my ways.

They were curious about what I thought about how people perceived me. They asked me questions and gave me an opportunity to figure things out for myself, and thankfully, they had enough patience with me to wait for me to see it. This leader wasn't even my leader. She was a subordinate to me. One time, after I told her about a negative situation, she asked, "Do you think there could be any other reason that it turned out that way?" Hurt, I said that I didn't know any other way it could have been. Months (literally) later, I reminded her of that conversation, and I asked her if she had something in mind that I may not have been ready to hear. She clarified her curiosity by saying, "Not at all. I was just curious if there was anything else that could have explained that situation better." It was truly her curiosity that helped me build myself into a different kind of person.

Is it easy to admit our weaknesses? No, it's not. And, often, we don't have to. When you are building someone instead of dissecting them, they don't need to be defensive about what is happening. That's incredibly powerful.

We need people to get better, but it doesn't matter much how they get better. And, what I've learned time and again is that they can get better without us telling them what to do but rather by asking questions of them. The power of questions is valuable in professional learning.

In his book *The Coaching Habit*, Michael Stanier discusses how powerful it is to ask questions. He gives several reasons why we stink at this and said, "The third reason is that the seemingly simple behaviour change of giving a little less advice and asking a few more questions is surprisingly difficult. You've spent years delivering advice and getting promoted and praised for it. You're seen to be 'adding value' and you've the added bonus of staying in control of the situation. On the other hand, when you're asking questions, you might feel less certain about whether you're being useful, the conversation can feel slower and you might feel like you've somewhat lost control of the conversation (and indeed you have. That's called 'empowering'). Put like that, it doesn't sound like that good an offer" (2016, pp. 6–7).

You see, the power of questioning is that you can ask a question and, to be honest, the response to you doesn't matter at all. Because it's not about you. It's about the person you're talking with. When you give someone advice, it's like giving them a hammer. They can use that hammer and see everything as a nail, but they probably won't. More likely, they will thank you for the hammer, show you they know how to use it, and then add it to all the other hammers in their drawer!

But when you ask a good, curious, well-intentioned question, it's more like revealing a whole work of art. When asked about finding a solution to AIDS, Dr. Jonas Salk, who is credited with discovering the polio vaccine, said this: "It comes from asking the right question, because the answer preexists…[the answer to polio was already there]…if you think of David and Michelangelo, it was in the stone, but it had to be unveiled, and revealed. You don't invent the answer, you reveal the answer" by asking the right question (CulturologyWorks, 2013).

The answer already exists, and the right question gets you to it. That may sound less scientific than we typically want to be in education, but it is the right approach. So, let's spend some time talking about the questions we should be asking as part of our observations.

Transforming Our Observations

Too often in education, we turn over decision making to those who are far away from the classroom.

Some of this is worthwhile, some is encoded into law, and another aspect is us just not standing up for what we truly believe.

Let's take the topic of teacher evaluations for a moment. Typically, in most schools, they have adopted one of a few options for teacher evaluation.

These carry names like Marzano and Danielson and others. Some districts even create their own, as my first district had done. But many are based on the work of Marzano and Danielson.

And why shouldn't they be? Danielson and Marzano have devoted their lives to helping develop teachers.

But they've done so in an attempt to "sciencize" the profession.

In his book, *10 Things Schools Get Wrong (And How We Can Get Them Right)* (2021), Dr. Jared Cooney Horvath said that each field gets to define its own evidence. Scientists use laboratory equipment to measure how things will work, but family practice doctors have to make decisions with the people in front of them.

In much the same way, academic researchers get to use studies and theories to make things work, but "in order for laboratory concepts to be practically useful within the classroom, teachers must prescriptively translate them to their unique context" (Cooney Horvath & Bott, 2021, p. 32).

"Evidence to a lawyer (e.g., precedent) is very different from evidence to an anthropologist (e.g., stories and myths). Evidence to a neuroscientist (e.g., blood flow) is very different from evidence to a psychologist (e.g., questionnaires). Importantly, none of this evidence is wrong, but it's only meaningful within the context" (Cooney Horvath & Bott, 2021, p. 33).

Jared suggests that teachers need to define their evidence. It cannot be defined by someone besides them. Although he's not arguing that teachers become scientific researchers, Jared is arguing that teachers "must methodically organize and collect information concerning the impact of varied practices within their classroom" (Cooney Horvath & Bott, 2021, p. 33).

So, what does this all mean? Let me list a few examples:

1. If you know that a student understands something but can't generate it in a testing situation, do they still know it?
2. If you as a teacher see that students are growing and changing because of a classroom discussion, is that evidence enough?
3. If you see that students are meeting the requisite standards but are not able to demonstrate it in a traditional way, is that evidence enough?

The answer to all these questions is YES!

Especially in my work with student driven learning, I've seen that there are many things that are not measurable on a test but are still incredibly worthwhile.

Allow me to share two small examples. First, one group of students wanted to create a social network for our school—run on our school devices, and bullying would be eliminated by design. This group of students never finished it, and because we focus on product instead of process in education, most educators look at this and say it was a failure.

Not so. These students learned high-level programming languages, learned how to conduct research, and learned how to save and share their work.

Second, a group of teachers decided to collaborate on a project among several different classes. Because of how our evaluation system was designed, in order for them to get high marks on their own evaluation, they had to stop the project and do teacher-led instruction with just their own kids in their own classrooms.

In other words, in order to maintain "highly effective" status, teachers had to stop doing highly effective activities and start doing meaningless activities that benefited no one except for them and only in the context of our evaluation system.

Needless to say, I wasn't going to ask them to stop building a rocket that would take them to Mars in order to demonstrate how well they could follow directions to put together an IKEA kitchen set.

Our teacher observations should not be done to benefit our evaluation system. Our teacher observations should be done to match the needs of our schools and our districts, not to "align" to best practices determined from some far-off place!

A teacher came to our school whom we knew we needed to "counsel out" within just a couple months. She was not right for our school but got great scores on the evaluation because she was a good teacher. Her "evaluation scores" were off the charts, but she was not happy and her kids were not happy.

According to the data, she should have stayed at our school. But looking at her, the kids, and her future, it was a bad idea. The data didn't support our decision, but we knew she couldn't stay at our building. Thankfully, we had the courage to recognize that she would not be well served by staying with us. We were happy to give her great recommendations to other schools, but it just wouldn't work with us.

Another teacher consistently did poorly on their teacher evaluation but was always the highest-rated and most loved teacher in our school. He didn't do well on the evaluation because he didn't teach in the way the framework said he should. He was completely unremarkable (only according to our evaluation system), but I hated to let him go to another school because he brought so much to our school and made us better.

These two outliers are certainly that: outliers. But they also underscore an important point. You can't base all your decisions on "research" or the "evidence" that someone else suggests. You have to look at your individual school and do what is best for it, even if it is not aligned with what the data say.

Trust Based Observations

When we seek to be curious, ask questions, and listen to what people in our school say, we not only get better results from our observations, but we also add to creating a culture that is supportive of everyone. Talking in episode 386, Craig Randall talks about trust-based observations. He shared, "The Gates Foundation had embarked upon a seven-year, $200 million research project to improve the quality of teaching, improve learning outcomes and graduation rates through basically the development of a more robust evaluation observation processes. And at the end of that, the RAND Corporation, who always comes in and evaluates these studies, came in and said that there really was *no sustained improvement in teaching learning or graduation outcomes* because of this." Even with all this effort, we still aren't having an impact. He said that when we start evaluating teachers, their creativity and risk-taking goes down. They want a good score, much like our students do.

In my first district, we needed to rate teachers on more than 60 indicators in each observation. Let me tell you, it was pretty much impossible to keep track of all that. Craig added that not keeping track is to be expected: "If you look at the research on observations and observation templates, it says anytime we have more than nine or 10 areas on an observation form, observers start to lose the forest for the trees. And so they ended up checking off boxes and not really noticing the teaching and learning."

You get so focused on checking the boxes, you forget about the thing most principals are there for: to improve teaching and learning. Craig highlighted the absurdity of teacher observations for evaluation purposes, "Because I mean, if you think about the vulnerability of teacher observation, what other job in the world has your boss come in to your so-called office, sit down, pop open a laptop, and watch you do your job 30 minutes. I mean, like, imagine if you were a barista and your boss walked in and sat behind the back counter and pulled up a chair and watched you. And they had all these numbers of indicators. It's really, really a vulnerable process for teachers. And so to have empathy for that, really, I think is important because as principals, sometimes we forget what it was like to teach, and sometimes we forget how hard it was. And so everything that we do in the reflective conversation and starting with we do the reflective conversations in the teacher's room."

It's very simple to implement. Using the 9 indicators he recommends, he encourages principals to do just 3 20-minute observations per day Monday through Thursday, and then have reflective conversations with teachers after that Tuesday through Friday. Rather than having a bunch of pre- and post-observation conferences and evidence evaluation, you get to just be in the classrooms and talk with the teachers. Because you are in the classrooms so often you see so much about what is happening. It's about building trust and helping teachers feel safe to take risks.

Craig is quick to encourage principals to not give feedback, as we've already discussed, but to note what teachers are doing, and then ask questions of the teachers. Don't offer suggestions to teachers, as it's not needed. He suggests the reflective meetings start our the same way, "it always begins with two questions. What were you doing to help students learn? And question number two is if you had to do over again, what, if anything, might you do differently?"

Note the difference in how the observation is approached. Rather than judgment and critique, the conversation is about the teacher's expertise and professional reflection. It's much easier for the principal to then support teachers when they are struggling, because they are much more likely to ask for help if you ask them what they would change.

Craig says, "teachers are frankly frustrated with the observation process and the fact that it does feel like a hoop jump. Many teachers now will say to me, I had my principal do the observation and they said, 'Everything was really great, except I didn't see such and such pedagogy. So next time, can you do that so I can mark it off?'"

Too often our observations focus on specific pedagogy and data collection. We need to de-sciencize the observation process and make it more about reflection. "And it's amazing," Craig says, "How much teachers appreciate just that you notice something in their practice!" Taking the time to notice the good things they are doing builds trust quickly.

Craig's program, Trust-Based Observations, has improved relationships, culture, and communication in the schools he's implemented it in. It's one way to be a transformative principal, and a good basis for the rest of the work transformative principals need to do.

Making Time for Observations

Geoff Woods, president of ProduKtive, whom we mentioned earlier, recognizes that the purpose of observations is to ensure that your vision is being met. He said, "For everybody who's listening to this as a principal, you have so many hats you have to wear, you have so many balls that are up in the air. What I love about what you've done, Jethro, is you started living the book. You got purposeful about saying 'this is the one thing: If I can just be in the classroom every day, that makes everything else easier or unnecessary.' And you prove to yourself that first and foremost, you're actually in control of your time. You've proved to yourself that by doing less, you can actually achieve more. And you've self-discovered that when you actually do narrow your focus, that all that 80% stuff, that everybody tells themself they have to do a lot of it, a lot of it just goes away or it doesn't matter." (https://www.transformativeprincipal.org/geoff-woods-tp-special-episode-1045/)

For me, when I made my one thing to get into classrooms every day, it made a ton of problems go away. If someone wasn't achieving the vision of our school, I could see it right there and address it. If someone wasn't living up to our culture, I could figure out how to help them make it better. If a teacher or student wasn't behaving correctly, I could address it right then and there.

In addition to these advantages, when I was out in the classrooms every day, the behavior issues decreased as well. The mere presence of the principal in the building encouraged everyone to live up to what they knew they should be doing.

It actually works.

Chapter Summary

Observations exist to help you determine whether your vision is being implemented in the school.

Observations by transformative principals fall in the second column below and build culture, relationships, improve communication and help people feel more supported in their role, all essential aspects we'll talk about going forward.

Before/Current	After
Transactional	Transformational
Feedback	Conversations
"Glows & Grows" (judgment)	Questions
Dissecting	Building
Evaluation	A

Key Questions

1. Are your observations based on trust, or are they based on compliance?
2. Is your feedback one-sided or do you have conversations?
3. Do teachers change their instructional strategies after your observations, or do they continue doing what they've always done? Do they need to change?
4. Think of the last 4 observations you've done. Could you see your Vital Vision implemented in those observations?
5. How long do you need to be in a classroom to see if your Vital Vision is being implemented?

References

Colorado Department of Education. (2014, December). *Educator effectiveness.* https://www.boarddocs.com/co/cde/Board.nsf/files/9RNMFV5B0E37/$file/1314%20Teacher%20pilot%20findings_SBE%20presentation_final.pdf

CulturologyWorks. (2013, March 7). *Dr. Jonas Salk on asking the right question.* [Video]. YouTube. https://youtu.be/eMFqqgsODRg

Consortium on Chicago School Research at the University of Chicago. (2007). https://consortium.uchicago.edu/sites/default/files/publications/07What Matters Final.pdf

Consortium on Chicago School Research at the University of Chicago. (2017). https://consortium.uchicago.edu/sites/default/files/publications/Predictive%25 20Power%2520of%2520Ninth-Grade-Sept%25202017-Consortium.pdf

Dumas, C. (2020). Let's put the C in PLC: A practical guide for school leaders. Next Learning Solutions Press.

Miller, D. (2009). *The book whisperer.* Jossey-Bass.

Scott, S. (2002). Fierce conversations: Achieving success at work & in life, one conversation at a time. Viking Penguin.

Stanier, M. B. (2016). The coaching habit: Say less, ask more & change the way you lead forever [Kindle edition]. Box of Crayons Press.

Sullivan, D., & Hardy, B. (2021). Who not how: The formula to achieve bigger goals through accelerating teamwork. Hay House Business.

Tableau. (2021a, May 5). *Enrollment by Fairbanks North Star Borough School District.* https://public.tableau.com/app/profile/k12northstar/viz/ Enrollment_1/Enrollment

Tableau. (2021b, October 22). *Graduation rates by Fairbanks North Star Borough School District.* https://public.tableau.com/app/profile/k12northstar/ viz/GraduationRates-by-School/Overall

CHAPTER SIX
Communication

The death of communication is the birth of resentment.

Dave Ramsey

We often refuse to accept an idea merely because the tone of voice in which it has been expressed is unsympathetic to us.

Friedrich Nietzche

If you want to kill any idea in the world, get a committee working on it.

Charles Kettering

An important part of leadership is recognizing that conflict always accompanies progress. Good leaders accept this and use it in achieving their goals.

Tom Hoerr, author of *The Formative Five* (2017)

Chapter Takeaway: Transformative principals have empathy and systematize communication.

Communication is not just about you speaking to others. In every conversation, there is a speaker, a receiver, and an unknown translator. Every additional participant in a conversation brings their translator with them. And we can't talk to or communicate or understand their translator. We can only hope that what we say will be understood how we intend it to be understood. That doesn't happen that often! So, we need to always go back and communicate again and again to make sure that people understand what we are truly trying to say. We also have to have patience when we see that someone is not understanding us. We may get sick and tired of saying things over and over again, but we still have to say them, repeat them, and reiterate them.

In this chapter, I'm going to talk about the importance of onboarding, specifically as it relates to families, but the idea extends to new employees and to students.

I'm also going to talk about empathy and conflict, and how to manage that.

Finally, I'll talk about communicating when you have pressure from all kinds of places to make a specific choice, and how you can communicate effectively under pressure.

Empathy

Adam Pisoni sold a product called Yammer to Microsoft for about a billion dollars. When I was invited to a dinner to learn about a new scheduling app he was creating, I thought, "this Silicon Valley guy is going to try to do something in education and it's going to be super lame." I was prepared for it to not meet our needs and to give feedback to make it better.

Well, I was very wrong.

Adam's demo and discussion of what ABL, Always Be Learning, his scheduling software, would do to our scheduling process was inspiring. He completely understood all the issues we were facing as school leaders with building schedules. After that demo, I knew this program was a game changer, and I later asked him what he did to make it so precisely fit our needs.

Rather than asking what's possible in schools, he asked what prevents traditional schools from becoming better. By asking that question, he was able to conduct empathy interviews with school leaders to see what wasn't working. Here's the big truth he found out and shared in episode 185, "Schools are being forced to lie to their systems to get their information correct."

For example, in my school, we had students all over the building in the classroom they needed to be in for what they were working on any given day.

Our student information system just could not handle that kind of approach. So, we knew that kids were in a different place, but the system thought they were still in a specific classroom. We could handle the changes, but the system couldn't, so we had to lie to the system in order to have our information correct.

After seeing the demonstration, I was eager to use it, and we were able to take our scheduling process from weeks to just a couple of days. It was amazing. And although Adam certainly spent the time and money necessary to develop a good product, it wasn't about that at all. It was about him really understanding what our challenges were as school leaders. It was about him gaining empathy with what we were facing and providing support directly to that end.

Empathy is where communication needs to start. Stephen Covey, author of *The Seven Habits Of Highly Effective People*, lists one of the habits as seek to understand first. He highlights the importance of empathy by helping us understand what the other person is experiencing.

High Tech High in San Diego has a good primer on how to conduct empathy interviews, which is essentially what Adam did with school principals in order to create ABL. High Tech High says, "Empathy interviews are designed to help individuals dig much deeper than the surface of 'How are you?' and the standard response of 'I'm fine.' It helps us identify not only the current state of students, but it also helps us gain understanding as to what our students' needs are and how we can support them."

They provide a process that is actually quite simple: Pay attention! It's a little more complex than that, but it involves observing the situation and then asking, "What are they doing?" "Why are they doing that?" "How are they feeling?" "How are they doing that?" These simple questions, when you take the time to think and reflect on them, can lead to all kinds of insights.

Eric Chagala (episode 251) is the principal of Vista Innovation Design Academy, a school that, without replacing any staff, completely changed how it delivered instruction. Eric's school went from being a traditional school to a heavily student-driven, design-thinking-oriented school. He and his staff spent time on empathy. They conducted empathy interviews.

Part of their process for conducting empathy interviews was to "listen deeply, and read between the lines of what people are asking for." Eric equated it to Steve Jobs knowing what people wanted when they could not articulate what they personally wanted but they knew it when they saw it.

This approach led to what Eric calls "turnaround kids." These are kids who were really struggling in a traditional model (getting in trouble all the time, bad grades, poor attendance) but then showed incredible skills when they were placed in a new environment. In the new school, these turnaround kids became the stars of the school when previously they were the duds.

Because they listened to what kids were struggling with, as they designed their new instructional approach, they found ways to apply what they learned in the empathy interviews and make school better for those kids, specifically, and by extension, every other student as well.

Empathy interviews are about asking the right questions to gain a deeper understanding of why things are happening the way they are. The empathy interviews don't do your work for you or solve the problem, but they do a much better job of identifying the problem. Eric said that it's vital that the interviewers "see what they [the subjects of the empathy interview] understand from the perspective they have" and that those who are conducting the empathy interview "have a really vast set of exposures."

It's not enough to ask just one or two people what is going on, but rather it is essential to dig deep and get the perspective of lots of people when you are redesigning a whole school.

This is the power of gaining empathy. It helps you understand the person deeply so that when you discuss the problems they are facing and offer solutions, your solutions are like the proverbial manna from heaven because they meet their needs so exactly.

Perhaps the best compliment I have ever received came from someone who read my book *SchoolX* (2020). He said, "If I were to write a book about education, it would be a lot like *SchoolX*. It felt like you were in my head."

Mark Modesti, a professional troublemaker and Customer Solutions Executive, talked about empathy in the 2016 Transformative Leadership Summit. He teaches us that empathy inspires creativity. The way I understand this is that if you can truly see the problems someone is facing, you don't have the blind spots that they do and you can much more easily find a solution to a problem because you are not bound by the challenges they face.

Perhaps a story will help illustrate the power of empathy. My daughter ran away while we were camping. She was supposed to just go to the bathroom, early in the morning, but instead went to go find someone. That's pretty scary to begin with, but it is scarier when compounded with the following factors:

- We were in Denali National Park.
- There were signs everywhere about a moose charging people if they got too close.
- There was a river not too far from our campsite.
- My daughter has no sense of direction.
- My daughter has no sense of consequences.
- My daughter is very stubborn.
- My daughter has Down syndrome and can't communicate very well to all people. We understand her, but not everyone else does.

I went to a place where I thought she might go. It was a place where she and I walked two days before, so it was possible she might know the way. I told the workers there the situation, including the above factors, and one worker's response was "Oh, just make breakfast. They usually come back when there is breakfast."

That one comment brought about so many emotions I could hardly stand it.

Anger—I was really angry that she would say something so insensitive. My daughter had no idea where she was or where we were. She has no sense of direction or ability to find her way back. She didn't know the name of the campsite where we were, only that we were in Denali. It wasn't just about breakfast. She was lost, and she would not miraculously find her way back.

Frustration—This person was not listening to me. She didn't understand my daughter! How dare she make some off-the-cuff response that totally disregarded all the information I had just given her about her disability and inability to find her way home.

Sadness—My daughter was lost, and nobody could tell me that she was going to come back home on her own. I needed help to find her, and someone who should have been able to give some help or advice on how to get help was completely unable to offer support.

Hurt—I felt like this person was judging me that I was upset that my daughter was lost. She seemed dismissive about what I was going through.

Empathy—I suddenly realized that this lady was totally unequipped to help comfort a parent who was in a dire situation. She didn't have the tools to help me be successful.

What does this have to do with education? I'll tell you:

1. We need to be supportive allies of parents. One of my friends asked me a while ago, "How can I be a good friend?" Many times, with parents, that's what we need to do.

2. We can't judge parents. Parents are likely doing the best they know how to do. We can't waste any time making judgments about what they are doing or how they can or can't do something. My daughter ran off through no fault of mine or my wife's. She had been to the bathroom at the campsite many times by herself, and she chose to run away rather than go to the bathroom. When that worker who should have helped me made me feel that way, I felt like I was a bad dad. I'm not. I'm not perfect, to be sure, but there was nothing I could do to have prevented it.

I really could have used some empathy. I really could have benefited from someone trying to understand how I was feeling in that moment.

Melissa Bernstein (episode 427) adds another element to this when she said, "If I were a principal, I would go into every classroom and I would tell a story to the kids and the teachers about when I was depressed, when I was anxious, when I was scared and how I had to use the tools in my own self to overcome that. And I still have times when I feel that way. And I want them to know as a principal, that it's okay to feel the full spectrum of emotion. It's okay to feel scared. It's okay to feel pressure that you might not do well, because I, as the leader of this school, feel it every single day as well."

Sharing this part of us helps us have empathy for others and what they're going through as well as helps us know how to support them when they share similar feelings.

Not only that, it also helps those who are struggling know that we could possibly have empathy for them! They could feel more accepted if we share some of our own struggles with them. They could be more willing to share if we have shared something about us first.

If we share our experiences with someone else who doesn't have those same feelings, they won't really care all that much. But those who are struggling will greatly appreciate what we have to offer!

Back to my daughter, because it would be tough to leave you without finishing that story! Once I realized that the worker I first talked to couldn't possibly have the tools needed to help me, I called the ranger station and talked to one of the park rangers. They said they had just received a call from someone saying that they had found a little girl almost two miles away from where we were camped. They had her and would meet us at a location closer to our camp.

Of course, my daughter was happy that she found some new friends and got to hang out and talk on a walkie-talkie, completely oblivious to the danger she was in and the fear she had created in us.

And this is where we need to talk about deeper empathy. After that incident, we had the conversation with my daughter that she can't run away. We learned something that we couldn't quite articulate for several more years, as she continued to run away. Every time she did, we would talk about how running away isn't good, and she has to stay with us.

We finally learned that she never saw herself as running away. She would never do that. She loves us. She wouldn't ever want to run away from us. In each of the times she has "left without permission or notification" she has always been going to find someone or something. In her mind, she was not running away. In our mind she was. In her mind, she was going to find her dad, or her friend, or food, or was going to school.

And here's the brilliant part, now that we have greater empathy for her, we know what questions to ask and what behaviors may precipitate what we would call running away and she would call going to find someone!

When I applied this same approach to dealing with students and teachers, my understanding of their motives for their behavior completely changed. I was able to see that they were not trying to rebel against me or the school, but were almost always doing the very best they could with what they had.

Gaining this deep empathy helps us forgive, coach, support, and enjoy our staff and students much more!

Onboarding Families

When we develop deeper empathy, it helps us communicate more effectively with the families in our schools as well. One area we don't give enough attention to is onboarding our families. Onboarding is teaching someone how things work at your school. If you're in a special kind of school that isn't a traditional school, you probably have to do something to help parents understand how things are different at this school. Well, even if your school is a very traditional school, the way you communicate your vision and values is through how you teach your families what your school is all about.

In this chapter, I'll share some strategies to make this effective. Some of them are small tweaks whereas others are actions you've probably never considered taking.

But first, what is onboarding? Onboarding is the process of helping people understand what you're doing. In episode 247 of *Transformative Principal*, Joe Erpelding said that onboarding documents a historical process of where we wanted to be. Onboarding processes are both practical and aspirational.

There are many ways to onboard, and you've probably done many of them: open houses, back-to-school nights, newsletters, robocalls, texts, emails, flyers, orientations.

Our goal for this section is to help you create a system of onboarding so that anyone who comes to your school can easily access the same information, whether they come at the traditional time or at any time throughout the year.

In order for your onboarding to work well, you have to have a good idea already of what your school is all about. You have to have a vision for your school. In order for your onboarding to work at all, you have to just do it!

Registration Process

Your school or district already has a registration process that you follow, but you still need to think about how this process works. One thing we're going to add here is how you collect and talk about the email addresses you are collecting. Your registrar needs to let parents know that they will be getting a series of emails explaining things parents need to know. The emails will come straight from the principal, and they will be full of information. The registrar should let parents know how many emails to expect and when they will get them.

Whatever the registration process is, it should also be something that is simple and clear for families. Make it easy on them. Then make it easier. No matter how easy you think it is, trust me, it is not as easy or as simple as you think. Depending on the complexity, you may choose that your registration process is "Give us your email and we will send you videos and instructions on everything!" Then those videos and emails would walk them through every step of the process.

One thing to consider: even if your school has been around for ages and you know how everything works, you still need to communicate it to people as though it is their first time.

When we moved to Spokane, Washington, my 6th grade son's big complaint about the school he was brand new to was, "It seems like they just assume that everyone has been here for the previous six grades. I haven't and I don't know how to do stuff!" He understood how lonely and isolating it feels when everyone assumes you know how to do everything.

Therefore, it's vital that you explain to everyone what you believe, how things work, and how to get help!

Onboarding Emails

Once you have parent email addresses, you want to start sending emails. I suggest using a tool like Mailchimp or Convertkit to send emails automatically in a way that does not require you to push any buttons! These are called *sequences* in many email programs. These allow you to set it and forget it. Once someone joins your email list, they get regular emails sent out at intervals to explain the onboarding process. If you can do this with text messages, that works too!

Here's how it works:

A parent submits their email. Your registrar inputs it into the automated email system. Without any further human action, it sends a series of 5–10 emails explaining how everything works at your school. The emails can include videos, images, links to specific web pages, and more.

The purpose is that these emails will be a tool for parents to know what to expect from your school. If appropriate, you can send these to students and to staff as well.

When I was a principal in Kodiak, Alaska, I sent these emails out to staff who were moving to our island. Moving to an island can be a big change for many people, especially to an island in the Gulf of Alaska. What we found was that it was beneficial for our emails to talk about island life and about school life. Understanding that it took about 2 months for most people to get to the island, we wrote a series of 10 emails, delivered weekly, to inform our staff about what they needed to understand.

A tip about onboarding emails: Don't talk about changes. Onboarding explains how we do things now. Don't get sucked into the trap of saying, "we used to do it this way, but next year things are changing."

At a middle school orientation I attended with my daughter, the school was going through some big changes. It was obviously unsettling to the teachers and specifically to the counselor who was leading the session. She said to this group of incoming seventh graders, "Next year, for you, we are going to have some big changes. We used to do things this way, but next year we are going to do things completely differently." Everyone left that orientation confused because we heard about two different ways to do things. What's worse, the school had a largely transient population, so of the kids who would be attending that school in the fall, nearly 70 percent of them would be brand new. The counselor wasted energy explaining how things were changing when it would have been much better to just say, "This is how it works here." You'll be tempted to discuss the way things used to work as well, but you've got to explain things as they are and as you hope them to be. People will largely live up to that expectation without much effort.

This is the power of onboarding. What you say as you teach people about the school are things they are more likely to remember. It doesn't mean it will be perfect, but you have historical documents to show what you aspired to be.

Conflict and Conscience

Even when we have already developed empathy, onboarded effectively, and communicated greatly, we are still going to have conflict. This is where most principals struggle. Transformative principals, however, approach these difficult conversations knowing they are a necessary part of being a leader.

In episode 449, I talked with Richard Shell, the Thomas Gerrity Professor of Legal Studies, Business Ethics, and Management at the Wharton School. He is the author of the book *The Conscience Code* (2021), and we talked about how to be a person of conscience.

Regardless of whether you are talking to a supervisor, subordinate, student, or stakeholder, it is vital to be a person of conscience. What does that mean? It means that you act on your values and do the right thing.

We did a little case study of a principal who was told to do something wrong for his school, and that principal needed to step up and say something.

Richard advised that the first step is gaining empathy and understanding why the superintendent was making the decisions he was making. The principal needed to seek to really understand the reasons behind the decisions.

Richard noted that there are five pressures people are under. You can remember them with the anagram PAIRS (peer, authority, incentives, role, systemic). Let's talk briefly about these.

Peer Pressure

Peers are adding pressure themselves. We often see this with teachers where they will act a certain way because their peers are pressuring them to act that way. Obviously, we see this with kids as well. And this is one that we all pretty intuitively understand. But there are a couple issues to pay attention to here:

1. Peer pressure is not always spoken.
2. Peer pressure can also be positive.
3. Peer pressure is not always easily identifiable.

I'll share a story to illustrate. When I was a first-year teacher in my first month of school, I was obviously struggling. I didn't know how to work with kids that well, and I was teaching mostly ninth-grade English. Some students were pretty disrespectful, and I didn't know how to handle it well. I figured out that if I gently put my hand on the forearm of a sitting student while I was talking with them, they would pay more attention. I shared this strategy at a faculty meeting about a month in and the room was completely silent. I didn't realize this was not appropriate to say in the faculty meeting, and the peer pressure was to knock it off! Nobody said anything to me, but the body language and the way people didn't respond to what I said made it clear that it was a bad idea to keep doing that. I do wish someone would have just said something. Needless to say, I stopped that behavior!

In another instance when I was a principal, a teacher got emotional telling her story of why she became a teacher and the rest of the faculty there showed positive peer pressure to encourage others to get real about why they became a teacher. This led to a really powerful conversation about how to help specific students and stopped the too-serious teacher from derailing the meeting as he was often fond of doing.

Authority Pressure

Authority pressure comes from the person in authority. In the case with the superintendent asking the principal to do something he knew was wrong, that position of authority was used to pressure the principal into doing it.

One of the most annoying things I hear from principals (and teachers) is, "I'm going to be a good soldier and if you say to do it, I'm going to do it because that's my job." This is an excuse to abdicate responsibility when you know that you are being asked to do something you don't agree with. It's not how transformative principals lead.

You must seek to do the right thing even if your boss is telling you to do something else. Rebuffing any of these pressures is difficult, but this one typically means you are refusing your boss, which could lead to you losing your job. However, as Richard said in episode 449, "Your values are only worth what you're willing to pay for them!" Sometimes, it could cost you your job.

I read an article during the pandemic that a couple members of an US Food and Drug Administration board were going to resign their positions in protest of the recommendation that people get booster vaccines. I don't know all the ins and outs, but resigning your position in protest takes you out of the conversation in the organization. If you're facing resignation or being fired, it's good for the resume to resign, I'll admit that. But if you resign, you are no longer going to be able to contribute to the conversation. That has to be part of the decision, also. Don't misunderstand me; there are more pressures.

Incentive Pressure

Getting money from a job is certainly incentive! And this is a perfect answer to why you may stay in a job: Making money to feed your family may be more important than this value that you have. Some things are more important than others. I knew a teacher whose husband had cancer and she was staying in her job, even though she didn't agree with many decisions being made, because it wasn't worth losing a job with the flexibility and the accrued sick days she had, and more. The incentives were putting so much pressure on her that she couldn't possibly leave that job.

But there are smaller incentives that pressure people to behave a certain way, too. It's not all life and death.

Incentives are different for different people, as well. My two youngest attend an elementary school where they have "Husky Bucks." My daughter can't wait to have the Husky Bucks, and she counts them numerous times and plans what she is going to do to get them, how she will spend them, and how much she should save.

My son, on the other hand, is completely not incentivized by them. He doesn't care at all whether he gets them, and he actually gets annoyed when someone writes his name on them because he likes to give them away.

I'm sure there's someone in his school who is also running some black market for Husky Bucks like there was at one of my schools.

It's also possible for incentives to combine with other pressures like authority or peer pressure. Having the admiration, respect, or acknowledgment of peers or authority figures could be part of it also.

Role Pressure

Role pressure can come from the role that you occupy. A superintendent has certain expectations put on her to do her job a certain way. So do principals and teachers. I have always hated doling out discipline, but my job as an administrator meant that I had great pressure to engage in that work even when I didn't want to. And who else was going to do it, anyway?

Systemic Pressure

Systemic pressure relates to what pressure the whole system is putting on people. Standardized testing is probably the best example of this in education. Nearly everyone decries standardized testing, but everyone does it because it is so systemic. Even people who vow to change it don't make much headway.

I was talking to a Pearson representative one time, and she said that Pearson takes its cues from the education system. She said that Pearson only has so much testing infrastructure because it's what the schools want. Many principals and teachers have blamed Pearson specifically for how much testing we do by assuming that Pearson is the one running the show, whereas they claim they are just responding to the needs of schools.

It is so systemic that both parties blame it comfortably on the other one!

Each of these five pressures is helpful in seeing what is causing us to act a certain way. The pressures can be good and bad. When they are good, we pretty much ignore them, but when they are pressuring us to act in a way that makes us not feel like a person of conscience, that's where we get into trouble.

If you are a principal and try to fight against a superintendent who is receiving systemic pressure, your cries will likely fall on deaf ears.

Here's an example. In 2016, there were a lot of changes in standardized testing. I was in Alaska at the time and very much not in favor of year-end testing. It was systemic, however, and complaining to my superintendent or school board would have been a waste of time. I needed to be true to my values, however, and I made the decision (because I was allowed to) of when we would test. I pushed it all the way to the latest days possible because I didn't want to have to deal with makeups for weeks (as I had the previous year) and I didn't want to be a guinea pig for a totally new system in its first year of implementation. From what I had learned already, the software was buggy, at times nonresponsive, and slow. So, our testing window was the whole month of March, and I elected to have my school test the last full week of March. That would give us two days to do makeups, which I thought would be sufficient.

We were also encouraged to do multiple practice tests to get the kids used to the system, but I agreed to just one practice test because that was the requirement.

I looked like a genius when a couple of days into testing, when a fiber-optic cable was severed at the hosting site and the tests were canceled for the whole state for the year. In reality, I wasn't a genius, I was just doing the best I could within a systemic pressure situation to maintain my values as much as possible.

Assuredly, that is all any of us can do when faced with that kind of situation. Maintain our values. Be people of conscience.

Three keys to dealing with conflict

How do we deal with conflict? As mentioned above, we need to start with empathy.

Then, we need to evaluate the pressures that could be causing someone to act this way.

Third, we need to address the issue. This is challenging, because conflict can hurt. Transformative principals don't avoid fierce conversations, because they know how powerful those conversations can be.

Each conversation is different, but there are three simple ways to do these conversations in a way that both people leave feeling as good as possible about it: State intentions, be honest, and give time.

These conversations can be with anyone, and this advice will hold true.

Before addressing any issues of conflict, it's wise to role play with someone you trust. Dr. Jeff Temple (Episode 437) is the Sealy and Smith Chair of Violence Prevention at the University of Texas Medical Branch, as well as a Licensed Psychologist and the Founding Director of the Center for Violence Prevention. His research focuses on the prevention of interpersonal, community, and structural violence, and has been funded through the National Institute of Justice, National Institutes of Health, and Centers for Disease Control and Prevention.

Dr. Temple suggests role playing to help yourself in this situation so you can be clear about what you need to get out of the situation. He says, "They role play by [talking to] each other about how they can resolve this misunderstanding or something so that [it is resolved] in a nonabusive, nonviolent way, and those role plays are extremely important because they get to practice it live. And so then when it happens in the real world, they've already practiced it."

You can role play with any of these situations and that helps you less emotionally involved in the outcome, regardless of what it is.

1. State intentions

Stating your intentions means not leaving ambiguity about what they're they for. Transformative principals clearly explain what they are intending the outcome of a meeting is.

"A person with integrity, capability, and results—but poor intent— would be someone who is honest and has capabilities and results, but whose motive is suspect. Maybe he/she wants to win, even at the expense of others. And others can sense that, and thus feel that they can't fully extend trust. On the other hand, a person of good intent without the other three cores (integrity, capability, and results) would be a caring person who is dishonest or cowardly with no developed talents or skills and no track record." (Covey, pp. 80). If your intent is stated clearly at the beginning of the meeting, you let people know where you stand and what is important.

Stating your intent is also a good barometer of whether or not you should have the meeting. Sometimes, you really shouldn't even bother with conflict if you don't have a clear intent for the conversation, yet. It's not good to stay in that position for long, but reacting too soon could cause problems that you aren't prepared to handle.

2. Be honest.

Honesty is not just about being direct, but also about recognizing the vulnerable positions that exist. It might be you who is being vulnerable. It might be the other person. Regardless, when you are honest in the conversation, you are going to be much more successful.

In addition, Stephen MR Covey explains it this way in his book *The Speed of Trust*, "It's possible to tell the truth, but leave the wrong impression. And that's not being honest." (Covey, pp. 64).

If you leave the wrong impression, say, for example that you let someone know their behavior is wrong, but that it won't lead to them losing their job, when you know that it will, that's not being honest.

You can still be kind while being honest. You don't have to yell and scream to communicate that something is not right.

3. Give time.

If you're calling a meeting, you've likely had more time to think about a situation than someone else. So be sure to give them time to process and think about it.

As leaders, we often overlook how uncomfortable it can be for someone to hear that they are not living up to expectations. I would suggest giving people time to process and think about the message that was delivered. That could be 2-3 minutes of silent time in the middle of a meeting, or it could be 2-3 days before a followup meeting.

On the other hand, if there's not a reason to belabor the point, don't do it. One time I had to fire someone. The conversation lasted no more than 5 minutes. It didn't need to be long, they didn't need time to process (at least not with me!), nor did we need to have a followup, but I did say in the meeting, "This is tough to hear, and I'm sure you'll have questions about everything. I will instruct the secretary to help you figure out everything that happens next, final paycheck, getting your stuff, and turning in keys."

Being able to have a short conversation and let them escape that awful position she were in was the best thing I could do for her. It was uncomfortable for both of us, but would have been even more uncomfortable if I had tried to give her time to process and ask my questions.

Using these three strategies of declaring intent, being honest, and giving time will help you resolve many conflicts and communicate more effectively, even when there's not conflict.

Chapter Summary

In every communication, speakers and hearers bring a translator through which they translate everything. Communication requires constant attention and care to ensure that each person is understood. While it takes time, the time spent is incredibly worthwhile.

Empathy is an essential part of communication. Stephen Covey called it seeking to understand before seeking to be understood.

Acting on your values and dealing with conflict is often a communication issue. State your intentions, be honest, and give people time.

Key Questions

1. Are you honest?
2. Are your intentions clear?
3. Do you give people time to process their work and practices?
4. Think of the last conflict you had, what made it challenging? What made it manageable?
5. Think of the last good communication you had, what made is so good?

References

Covey, S. M.R. (2006). The SPEED of Trust: The One Thing that Changes Everything (p. 117). Free Press. Kindle Edition.

Hoerr, T. R. (2017). The formative five: Fostering grit, empathy, and other success skills every student needs. ASCD.

Jones, J. (2020). SchoolX: How principals can design a transformative school experience for students, teachers, parents—and themselves. John Catt.

Lencioni, P. M. (2012). *The advantage: Why organizational health trumps everything else in business.* Jossey-Bass.

Shell, R. (2021). *The conscience code: Lead with your values, advance your career.* HarperCollins Leadership.

Woods, G. (Host). (n.d.). *The ONE thing* [Podcast]. https://www.the1thing.com/podcasts/102/

Woolsey, R. (2016, March 30). *Severed internet cable interrupts-student testing in Alaska.* KCAW.org. https://www.kcaw.org/2016/03/30/severed-internet-cable-interrupts-student-testing-in-alaska/

CHAPTER SEVEN
Relationships

If the creator has a purpose in equipping us with a neck, he surely would have meant for us to stick it out.

Arthur Koestler

The reason why men always failed to establish important measures was because in their organization they never could agree to disagree long enough to select the pure gold from the dross by the process of investigation.

Joseph Smith

Standards without consequences are merely suggestions.

Gene Rivers

Standardization might make sense for manufacturing car parts or computers, but it does not work well for developing human beings.

Charles G. Koch

Chapter Takeaway: Transformative principals build positive relationships and empower their staff members to build positive relationships with all students and parents.

Jevon "JT" McCormick's mom was a sex worker and his dad was a pimp. Pretty inauspicious way to start out, right? Well, Jevon didn't let that stop him from being successful. He is a millionaire now, and he runs a multi-million-dollar business helping authors write their books. He's amazing and inspiring.

When I had the chance to interview him (episode 234) and learn his story, I was sure there was a teacher somewhere that helped him find the path to success. I couldn't wait to hear his response. In fact, I was wrong. He shares his story: "You know, even when you asked me the question, I have certain teachers. I remember just because we all have those individuals we remember, but not anyone I would say who was incredibly influential, who pushed me. I don't have that motivational story of, 'Oh, there was this teacher, she stood by me and she took me the extra mile.' Or 'This teacher, he was always there for me.' I don't have that story."

That's the story that they would have made a movie about. Think about that. Jevon went through 13 years, and at least twice that many teachers, and not one of them built the kind of relationship with him that we always say we should all have with all students.

Jevon continues, "I was pushed through a bad educational system in Dayton, Ohio. And when I got to San Antonio, Texas, my sophomore year of high school, I had shared with you that my mother took me to enroll into the high school and the counselor says, okay, you're in 10th grade, you should be in geometry. And truth be told that was the first time I'd ever heard the word geometry, let alone know what this class was going to consist of. That was the first time I heard the word. Six weeks into it at this new school, people found out quickly I wasn't a bright child and they tested me and I was testing on a fifth or sixth grade level, but here I was in 10th grade geometry as a sophomore."

He languished until the end of his senior year, without enough credits to graduate, a young man just being pushed through the system.

We often take for granted that there's a teacher behind those inspirational stories of success. But in Jevon's situation, there wasn't a principal or a teacher who made an impact on him.

Think about your school. Does every student have a trusting adult? Did Jevon have a champion, as Rita Pierson (2013) admonishes in her famous TED Talk? He sure didn't. Do your students? What about the ones who are quiet, shy, and don't have much to say? What about those who come from a great family and have every privilege? They need relationships too.

When I got married, I received some advice that if I thought of our marriage as an equilateral triangle, with me at one point, my wife at the other, and God at the third point, it would help our marriage. I didn't really understand it then, but the key point was that if we were not selfish, thought of others, and had a higher purpose, we would be better overall.

What I learned that is applicable here is that if you have a reason for working with someone on something, you're going to be better equipped to handle it if that common goal focuses your efforts.

Eric Makelky (episode 457) is a principal in Pinedale, Wyoming. He's in the middle of a sparsely populated state but understands the power of relationships. One of his regular goals is to ensure that "Every student who walks in the school can identify by name one trusted adult." When he first started, the perception of his teachers compared to the perception of his students was shocking!

He says, "When we first measured it, asked the students, do you have a trusted adult? If so, who is it? 31% of our students said they do. Then I asked the staff, what percent as a staff member, do you think what percent of our students do have at least one? Staff said 99%."

Going back to Jevon's story, he didn't have any one teacher or principal who he would consider a trusted adult. In Eric's school, only 31% said they did, when teachers thought 99% of students did.

Eric continues, "Well, We got better. We got better. We finished last school year with a new record. 97% of our students had a trusted adult they could identify."

So, that may be 97% of students, but there's still 3% of students who 100% don't have an adult they can trust.

But what is it like in your school? Do students have trusted adults? Do staff members have trusted leaders they can turn to? Do families have trusted staff members they can turn to?

Transformative principals build positive relationships and empower their staff members to build positive relationships with all students and parents.

Why do we build relationships?

It's important to have those relationships, but why do we have them? Well, we know relationships help us do lots of things, but we often overlook one of the major reasons for having a good relationship. The research has shown there are three big reasons for having relationships: care, candor, conflict. Geoff Woods is the cofounder and president of ProduKtive, a business coaching organization founded on the principles of *The ONE Thing* book by Gary Kellar and Jay Papasan that I mentioned previously. Geoff understands the power of relationships and what they can mean for our life and our success. In episode 1045 (a special episode), he said, "You can have everything you want in life, if you just help enough other people get what they want first. You want to build that relationship. You want to be the type of person who can bring candor and care to the table, to the relationship."

In this specific instance, he was talking about having difficult conversations with a teacher who isn't doing well with students. You want to bring candor and care to the table. That is the power of what we do. Relationships are about seeing each person as an individual. They are about meeting them where they are. It means understanding what they need and adapting ourselves to them.

In the final chapter on culture, I'll talk about Amy Fast's approach with her students. Because she wants every single student to know that she understands and cares about each of them, they feel like they are the most important person in the room when they are with her. That's powerful. That's building powerful relationships. This is where the domino effect really comes into play. When you have candor, care, and conflict through relationships, building culture becomes much easier.

Zaretta Hammond, in episode 157, explained why we have that relationship: "And the reason that we build that relationship is so that when learning gets hard, we have the relationship so that when that push is needed, the teacher can push the student." This is the candor that is needed in relationships.

But it's not just about when the learning gets hard. It's when anything gets hard. And there is a lot that is hard in schools. It relates to relationships between teachers, students, principals, and community members. Everyone. Zaretta continued,

When that push is needed, the teacher can push the student without the student falling apart, without the student being

resistant. But the student looks at the teacher and says, you've got my back. You're actually pushing me because you care for me. And information processing ease is what we're really trying to do is really trying to get the student to process the content that's being taught in new ways.

I want you to suspend your belief for a moment that "being taught" means in the classroom setting with the teacher lecturing. There are many ways to be taught something, and they don't just happen in formal learning environments. You know as well as I do that teachable moments occur everywhere and are actually remembered more than formal learning events.

And, as Gina Rodriguez (episode 438), principal in El Paso, Texas said, the learning falls into place when the relationships are taken care of.

Tony Sinanis (episode 20) shared that one of the things that has helped him create positive relationships with his community is his use of social media. He said that by sharing part of who he is as a person, it makes for a powerful way to show others that you are still human. You're not supposed to share just to brag, but you share to build relationships. He said that he doesn't do his job for the glory (little though there may be) but rather for the people he is serving: "I come here because I want to set the stage for other people to shine and for other people to grow and for other people to learn and my job is to remove the obstacles, not be the obstacle or not be the focus … And again, it's not about you. It's about the relationships you build and it's about not taking yourself too seriously." He shares care for his community by putting them first, and helping them see who he is as a person as well.

He said that when you project yourself like you have it all figured out, you project that you are finished learning. But more important, you need to be constantly learning. People don't always want to tell the principal if they're wrong, but it is a necessary step. Tony continues, "I was totally open to, 'Hey, tell me, rip me apart. Tell me why this does not work. Because I don't know.' What do I know? I only know from the experiences I have. The smartest person in the room is the room, right?"

Three superintendents in Chicago, Michael Lubelfeld, Nick Polyak, and PJ Caposey, took this to the next level by writing a book called

The Unfinished Leader (2021). Nick said in our interview (episode 414), "When you think about coaching and leadership development there's a misnomer that's at the heart of what we were trying to get through: we hear people talk about trying to be the best version of themselves. There's no such thing as the best version of yourself. There's only the next version of yourself. We want to help people understand that it's this continuous journey of always getting better because even the challenges we're trying to meet are changing as we're trying to meet them."

When you recognize that you are an unfinished leader, and you project that to others, it builds your credibility and relationships with others. When people think that you have everything figured out, they're not interested in engaging.

One superintendent, Gregg Taylor, did me a huge favor early in my career. I was on an interview with him, and there were a bunch of other people interviewing for this same position. I was the youngest and least experienced person, but he liked what I had to say in my application so he wanted to interview me, and he thought maybe I had what it took.

Well, I didn't get the job, and when he called to tell me (which was another solid relationship-building strategy), he shared with me that part of the reason I didn't get the job was that I appeared to know how to do everything and that I already had all the answers. I asked him, "Well, isn't that what you want? Isn't that what we should be striving for— knowing what to do?" He calmly listened to my question and then taught me a valuable lesson. "Jethro, if people think you have all the answers, they won't believe that you'll be open to their answers. Yes, you need a broad knowledge base. Yes, you need to understand things. But if you go into a meeting with someone and you already have it all figured out, what is the point of meeting with them in the first place?" In building a relationship in a short period of time through a phone call to tell me I wasn't getting a job, he took advantage of the opportunity for candor to help me learn what I needed to learn.

This was hard to hear for my young mind, but it was very valuable and it helped me know how to approach situations in the future. As leaders, we need to project that we aren't done growing. We need to be open to feedback from others, and that will help us have success.

Why would you take the time to build a relationship if you aren't going to use that relationship in the most positive, and productive way possible. A principal I work with was struggling with an employee that she had grown very close to over the years. This employee, we'll call her Sandra, was overweight, smoking, had health issues, and those health issues started impacting her work. The principal, we'll call her Jane, said, "I guess I'll have to stop hanging out with her and unfortunately, I'm going to lose that friendship."

What is the purpose of building the relationship if you can't have the hard conversation with someone that you love? Why focus on relationships if you can't have that candor that is needed? We need to be comfortable with conflict, as I addressed in the previous chapter.

I encouraged Jane to talk with that employee as a friend and as a boss, but to ensure that she put the relationship first. Jane said, "Well, I can't tell her to stop smoking because I'm her boss, and that's not my place!" But it is her place as a friend. Jane was avoiding the conflict, but it needed to happen. She admitted that she knew it would be worse if she started giving Sandra the cold shoulder and that would create greater conflict.

Jane decided she would try it, and she talked with Sandra. She told her she cared deeply about her and wanted her to be happy and healthy. As her principal, she was concerned about the days of work she was taking off, as it was impacting everyone else. As her friend, she was more concerned about her weight and her smoking. Jane reported that this was a tough conversation, but that Sandra really appreciated Jane's care and candor. This difficult conversation not only got the issues Jane was concerned about out on the table, but it also helped deepen their relationship!

I once had a boss who said that people should stop talking about their lives outside of work in the hallways. She was so focused on instructional improvements that she truly said, "Instead of asking a teacher how her weekend was, principals should be asking how that last assessment went and how the kids did." Not only did she turn her employees off by saying that, she also discouraged us from building a relationship with her, and ensured that none of us would ever go to her with help with anything, because she only cared about results. She was only about the conflict.

Delilah

Another person who was only about the conflict was Delilah (not her real name). Delilah was to me a classic "Chicana gang banger"—Huge hoop earrings, poofy hair, big curly bangs. She knew violence and carried it on her persona every day. Only difference was, she was almost 50 years old. But she still carried the look and attitude of the kids I grew up with in southern California. It was my last week at the school, and she was sad to see me go. She gave me a big hug and thanked me for everything. This was a much different reaction than I got in our first conversation nearly three years previous.

Delilah had a childhood similar to Jevon: troubled, lots of moving, early exposure to situations that put her in danger. She was now a grandma. Her life led her to join a gang in southern California, spend time in prison, and then end up as a grandma at just under 40 years old. She was now taking care of her 10- and eight-year-old grandsons while their mom was in prison. She didn't want this life, but it was what she had. She wanted better for her grandsons. But she'd been angry and fighting against the system for so long that any sign of authority was a symbol of the oppression that she believed had held her down for so many years. It was a symbol of the trials she had faced and the unfair treatment she had endured. Her boys knew that grandma could get fired up if they claimed they were being treated unfairly, so guess what they did in every situation? They pitted their grandma against the principal time and time again. I came in as assistant principal, not knowing any of this, and immediately got suckered by these two boys, which ended with Delilah yelling at me and threatening my life.

What turned the tide for us happened almost by accident. One of her boys had gotten into trouble and we were dealing with it. She came in hot and was ready for a fight with me. As was always the case with her, when one of the boys was in trouble, she refused to talk on the phone and she would come in. Something was different this time, and her grandson was not acting how he usually did. I perceived that he was being blamed for something somebody else did. She would hear nothing of it on the phone, and Carlos (also not his real name) was in the office when I called her. I decided to wait outside for Delilah to get there. She got out of her car and stomped up to me, but she wasn't in a fighting stance yet. When she was about ten feet away, I said, "I don't think Carlos did anything wrong."

She was surprised to see me and more surprised to hear what I said. She eyed me suspiciously and asked what I was talking about. I told her he was acting differently, and the way kids were acting in the class looked different than usual. I had always tried to be fair with Carlos and his brother, but they did get in a lot of trouble and that made it difficult to give them the benefit of the doubt. Carlos was still waiting in my office, and I asked Delilah if we could try to get it out of him. She said she would go talk to him in private and figure out the story. I let her into my office and gave them a few minutes. They talked it over; this was a small infraction anyway, but because Carlos was in trouble all the time, it was routine at this point for him to go to the office, and he didn't mind not having to be in class. While she was talking to him, I went and found a reliable student and asked him what happened. Away from his peers, he let on that Carlos hadn't been the instigator but did get blamed for it. And nobody wanted to tell on the other boy because nobody wanted to cross him. Carlos always got in trouble anyway.

I joined Delilah and Carlos in my office, and Delilah and I teamed up to support Carlos. In that moment, everything changed. Delilah no longer saw me as the adversary. She saw that I was focused on helping her grandson and she started to trust me. She started to believe that I could do what was right for Carlos. We got that situation resolved, and that was the first time that Delilah had ever felt like a school official cared about her family. I like to think that I approach every situation caring about the family, but when Delilah and I worked together to help Carlos, she saw that there was care for her and her grandson. Not every relationship with a parent has worked out that way for me, but that was a clear example of the advice I had received playing out. When we see ourselves as a team, working together, we can build relationships fast.

Crisis and Shared Beliefs

Delilah was almost always in crisis, but when we shared our focus and attention on helping her grandson, she was very willing to work with me, rather than against me. Tom Mahoney (episode 369), a superintendent in Chicago, suggests that we build relationships around shared beliefs.

Tom mentioned that his role as a leader, and even as a human being, is so much more than just living. He said, "My, my role here, my job on earth is not to find happiness, it's to find opportunities to be of service," and the added benefit is that when you are in the service of others, that does lead to happiness.

Tom also recognizes that sometimes we are not our best selves, especially when we are in crisis mode. He has a powerful way of helping people deal with that. He said,

> When we're in crisis, we really go back to our lizard brain. Right? We're in survival mode a lot of times. And so, when I talked to my leaders, I talked to them most of the time about taking first taking care of themselves and not allowing themselves to be controlled by the urgent. The second thing we talk about is this idea that you have to invite that person out of that place. No one is staying in a place of crisis because they want to be there. They just don't know how to get out! So, we talk a lot about this idea of trying to frame things different for teachers, and then trying to invite them out, literally saying to them, "Hey, would you be open to a different possibility on how to deal with this situation?"

You have to have the courage to invite people to move out of the crisis they are in. Often, people feel safe in the crisis they are in because they know it. But more important, they are often afraid of the change that must happen to get out of that crisis situation.

Gina Rodriguez (episode 438) has dealt with a lot of crises in her school in El Paso—from a Walmart shooting, to a community member being killed in her parking lot, to student deaths, to the border crisis essentially in her backyard. But what she has learned is that through building relationships, you can help people with any of those crises. She has sound advice as it relates to reacting to crises in powerful ways: "As a principal, you need to treat every situation as if they were your family member or your really good friend. Well, how would you react to the situation if it was a family member or if it was a girlfriend's family member?

I think that that's how we need to lead, because it puts that heart component into leadership and it brings that caring component."

The community can easily look at the position of principal as one that is focused just on managerial issues or curriculum. But when the principal acts like everyone is a member of her family, it changes things. Gina continued, "When you start putting all those blocks together and really take care of that, then the grades and the learning just really falls into place more easily."

What a marvelous way to look at things. Gina also shared how people have reached out to her when she's gone through these crises. A look, a soft touch, a hug, a prayer medallion left with a note—all those little things endear her to others and make what she's going through easier to bear. And, when you lift up others, it makes your burdens seem lighter as well.

Bullies

Despite our best efforts, there are still times where someone is not going to reciprocate our earnest endeavors at building relationships. Difficult as this may be, it's going to happen from time to time. Just because we are educators doesn't mean we are immune from this. In fact, some would argue that our educational system actually breeds bullies. When people are in crisis, have had bad experiences in the past, and don't know how to manage their own emotions, it can lead to them acting like bullies.

It is something that we almost never talk about. But many of the principals and leaders I have interviewed have shared how this peer bullying by teachers and principals does occur all the time. We need to be aware and proactive about how to deal with it.

I interviewed Brian Costello (episode 101) about this very thing. He noted that people in education can be super patient with kids, but then when it comes to adults, some people really struggle to have patience. When he shared something about a certain teacher, just talking about her would make his heart rate increase. The teacher would come into a room and would yell and scream and berate another teacher for whatever mistakes they had made. It got to the point in the school where everybody just ignored her behavior. The bullied teacher "just sat there and listened because where else are you going? What else are you going to do? People learned to just ignore her and go about their business, because she was going to come in and rant and rave. And if you disagreed with her, then she'd just be mean to you." I've seen this type of behavior in many schools. Sometimes, it's the principal who is acting that way, and sometimes it is a fellow teacher or other staff member.

You get what you tolerate in a school, and in Brian's school that's what everyone tolerated, so that is what they got.

Brian stood up to this bully, and the reply that he got from her was that she felt threatened because of what he said. His principal, on the other hand, thanked him for standing up to the teacher bully and appreciated what he said and how he said it. He had written her an email (because he didn't feel safe talking to her in person) saying that how she was treating others was professionally discourteous.

I asked him how he found the courage to stand up to her when so many others had not. He said, "My thought was, I mean, I could say nothing, but then what happens next? Is she going to keep doing this to me? For some reason I all of a sudden ended up in the crosshairs and for really no reason, it was a simple mistake that could have been skipped over and I could have come back and fixed it."

Brian showed that he wouldn't tolerate bullying and he made efforts to fix it and not have it continue, at least not when he was around.

This is the devious side of this kind of behavior; people will do it in secret or away from those who stand up to them.

Transformative principals tackle this head on. We aren't afraid of the conflict and know that we need to say something.

One principal asked me not to share too many details of this situation after we talked on the podcast, but that I could share an anonymized version of it. A teacher who was in a position of leadership within the union berated another teacher. If a principal had done that, everyone would have gone crazy at how disrespectfully the principal was acting. But, because this person was in the union, he was basically untouchable. He had used his union position several times to bully and demean others, and the previous principal had allowed it, being afraid to be seen as "going after" the union leader. Well, this new principal, we'll call her Robin, would not tolerate that. She reprimanded the union leader for his behavior and said that if she heard any word spoken about it to the person who reported it, she would write him up again for retaliation. Robin said an appropriate response would be a letter of apology, and anything else she would count as retaliation. This was a bold step for Robin to take, and she said it nearly started a retaliation complaint against her from the union leader. What it boils down to is petty, childish behavior. It's not acceptable, and kudos to Robin for standing up to that teacher. Even though this relationship was fraught with challenges, Robin was clear that negative behavior wouldn't be tolerated and her staff appreciated that she took that step. Even the union leader was appreciative, in his own way, of how the principal handled the situation.

Rick Jetter and Rebecca Coda (episode 194) call it the School Leader's Dunk Tank. As the leader, you are sitting in one of those old carnival games where someone gets to throw a ball, and if they hit the target, it drops you into a big bucket of water. As the school leader, you are often sitting there minding your own business, not even aware of what is about to happen, and then BAM! You are in the drink. These shots can come from peers, teachers, community members, or supervisors.

Rebecca suggested listening to your gut to know if it's coming from your supervisor. She said, "You gotta listen to that voice when it comes by, because your intuition is typically right on. So, when you notice behaviors, things, even the smallest things like, you know, cliques, whispering, or it could be something as big as sabotage where you're all of a sudden given 10 projects and you're already working 14-hour days. And you know, you can't do them, but you know, you were given the project so that you would fail."

It's hard to feel that people are setting you up to fail, but it happens. It comes down to relationships. She continued, "If you've had a very amiable professional working relationship with somebody, and then all of a sudden you notice the behavior of people around you change. You notice things showing up on your calendar or you notice emergency meetings or you notice you're not included or you're excluded from certain things." Earlier in the chapter, this is essentially how Jane wanted to resolve the situation with her secretary who was having health issues. She wanted to sever the relationship and start working on getting the secretary out. That's not the right approach.

Although these things will happen, it's important that you prevail instead of drown in these situations. The advice they give is excellent regardless of where the pressure is coming from.

First, you need to depersonalize the situation, which is so difficult when you are in the middle of it. Rebecca said, "So anytime that we can depersonalize the situation, as hard as it is, and it's the hardest thing to do when it feels personal. But if you can, even for a moment, and step away from it, that's just the beginning of prevailing."

Depersonalizing is tough, but here's a way to approach it. Take the advice of Gina Rodriguez and ask yourself how you would handle the situation if instead of you it was a family member in that situation.

The next step Rebecca mentions is what Brian did. Use your voice! Speak up and say something. Do it professionally, don't stoop to their level, but be clear and unafraid of the conflict. Rebecca shared the story of a friend who used her and then completely dropped her when she got what she wanted. Rebecca said, "Hey, you know, I really set you up for success. I put my name on the line to get you over here. I believed you. We worked really well together. I saw you grow and master these things, and I really expected that you were going to have integrity and a strong moral compass. And you know what? It just makes me feel terrible about myself and embarrassed that I brought you over to see you act so childishly and take advantage and not have a strong work ethic."

But Rebecca was quick to point out that things would have been better had she said something earlier instead of letting it fester.

Rick shared a story about a reader of their book who was getting blitzed by her superintendent and principal while she was an assistant principal. She used her voice to say, "This is how you're making me feel. You are making me feel irrelevant here. And I want you to look at this [book] so that we can work together to help our students."

And she walked out of the office and left Rick and Rebecca's book there. Rick finishes the story, recognizing that the principal may not have actually read the book, but "he certainly flipped through it because later that month he went up to his assistant principal and he said, 'You know what, I'm being a jerk. I've been a real jerk to you.' And he said, 'Let's try to figure this out.'"

There is power in depersonalizing, using your voice, and of course practicing what you're going to say so that you're not on the verge of tears as you say it.

Finally, it doesn't always work out positively. I had an experience where once I got on my supervisor's naughty list, and she just stopped talking to me. And she hasn't talked to me since. She wasn't bullying me, but our relationship deteriorated rapidly. She assumed that I was doing something wrong, and wasn't interested in listening to me explain it or describe how what I was doing was completely in line with our current policies. It was, in my mind, a misunderstanding. That can happen also, but I don't begrudge her that. She has different experiences, information, and expectations than I do, and it didn't work out. I still respect her and would be open to chatting with her anytime she wanted.

When it comes to relationships, transformative principals take the high road. They are humble, teachable, patient, and willing to be wrong. But it doesn't mean they are a doormat for the people with whom they are butting heads.

It isn't always easy, though. One person really betrayed me and when she tried to reach out later, it was really uncomfortable. I didn't know why she had acted that way with me before, so I found a way to make that conversation work out using advice from Melinda Miller.

Assume Positive Intent and Three Other Strategies

Relationships can sour, turn cold, or end. There is a way to deal with all of this. Melinda Miller is one part of the dynamic duo that inspired me to start a podcast to begin with. I was fortunate to interview her in episodes 10 and 11. She is a great principal who has done so much to help others and build relationships for years. She is still someone I feel like I can call up at any time and ask any question, and she would be there for me. Isn't that a great reputation? I admire her so much.

She gave some great advice. "Most people aren't doing things to be spiteful. I assume positive intentions." When someone doesn't get something done or otherwise doesn't do something perfectly, she knows that it wasn't on purpose, it was just, as she said, "They forgot they needed my help, so I ask, 'Can I help you with this?'"

It's a great strategy for always building relationships.

At the time of this writing, more than 110 episodes of *Transformative Principal* address the need for building relationships. Melinda's suggestion about assuming positive intent is one of the best ways to build relationships.

Another great tip comes from Will Parker (episode 76), where he shared another way he builds relationships. He doesn't share negative experiences with anyone. He keeps it close to his chest. As my friend for several years, I've only seen him be true to this principle. He said, "I value the relationships with my staff and my team members so much that it's kind of like, I don't talk about the conflicts I have with my kids or my wife. Now, I may tell you the lessons I've learned in those situations, but I'm not going to air anything that would embarrass anyone or would divulge confidentiality."

Will and I have both shared, numerous times, lessons we have learned, but I have not heard Will talk negatively about anyone, even when I knew it would have been warranted. That's the kind of integrity we want to have.

Teri Barila (episode 178) founded the school that was featured in the movie *Paper Tigers* (2015). The school is a trauma-informed school, and they seek to deal with trauma first rather than as an afterthought. It's an alternative school, and they know that pretty much everyone has experienced some form of trauma.

Teri said that the key to building relationships, especially with kids who have been impacted by trauma, is for adults to build skills in regulating their own emotions. She said, "The number one strategy really starts with building adult skills and capabilities to then affect the child's outcomes. It starts with making sure that we are able to regulate even in that moment of stress. If we don't, we are modeling the wrong thing and those mirror neurons, if you guys know about the mirror neurons and how the kids mimic, what they see when sometimes we're not even aware of our body language or our stance or that look, you know, the look."

Relationships with other people are stressful. If you can control your body language, your face, and your expressions, you're going to be in a much better position to build a relationship rather than tear it down.

Another strategy to forge relationships builds on what Theresa mentioned. Be visible! Make sure that people see you and have the opportunity to talk with you and get to know you better. In the previous chapter, Zaretta Hammond (episode 157) taught us about trust generators. What gets measured gets done, and Zaretta encourages us to measure and pay attention to relationships. She calls them "learning partnerships, where there's trust between the student, that the teacher is holding the student to not just high expectations but is able to kind of push the student into their zone of proximal development." When you, as the principal, observe, comment on, and articulate why it's important to have learning partnerships in the classroom, you'll start to see it happening more. And remember, you can't talk about those things if you aren't doing it yourself by being out there in the classrooms and talking about those same things with your teachers and having a learning partnership with your teachers.

Another strategy comes from Baruti Kafele. He said, "Consider how the day starts. Is there somebody out there greeting those kids in the morning, meaning the principal, making sure that that kid feels welcomed into the school each and every day?" Part of being visible means being out there in the morning greeting your students and making sure they feel welcome at your school.

These strategies, assume positive intent, having integrity, regulating your own emotions, and being visible all will help you build relationships in powerful ways. But there is an additional skill that is powerful for helping you build relationships that last a long time.

Gratitude

Showing gratitude is one of the most powerful things you can do. Katharine Birbalsingh (episode 368) is principal of the Michaela School in London. She talked about giving people opportunities to feel your gratitude. It's so important for them to know that you appreciate what they are doing for your school.

Justin Thomas (episode 383) encourages us to look for someone to whom to show our gratitude. He said, "Tomorrow, when you go to work, say thank you to somebody who no longer hears it because you're so accustomed to them being so automatically good that it's become no longer necessary to say."

We often overlook those who don't cause drama and are just everyday heroes for the work they do. Justin continued:

So, if it's somebody who's never near the drama, somebody who always has their attendance in on time, somebody who, they're just solid instructionally, great with parents. And you spend no time on them because they don't need you. Just pull them aside, either look them in the eye in person or put it on a sticky note (stationery is better) but [tell them], "I see you. I recognize you. I appreciate this specific thing that you do continuously. It matters so much and you make a tremendous difference.

And we can't forget that as principals, assistant principals, even teacher colleagues, people love to be recognized. They won't ask for it. They will never confess to you that it feeds them, but it's a tremendous difference-maker.

A transformative principal is giving gratitude to others every single day. It's so important. Whatever you can do to express your gratitude will be recognized and appreciated.

I spoke with Michelle Mann in episode 379, and she shared a story of a young man who had a standoff with police at the age of 14. She reflected, "We never know a person's potential. I may be able to see all the things you've done, but I don't know your potential. It is for me to pour into you. And I believe that, you know, just that seed of self-worth and him getting those accomplishments and understanding what it was like to, just to succeed without the criminal activity."

We don't know their potential, but we can still help them live up to it no matter where they are. Michelle continued, "I took him to Tennessee to the Department of Juvenile Justice national convention, and he was a speaker, and he told his—it was really his testimony. And I think that when you have situations like that, it also reaffirms, just the gratitude of really pouring into the lives of others and how you can help them."

This young man can never pay her back for helping him get away from a criminal life, learn a trade, and find a wife who would love him. But Michelle understands his gratitude for her because she regularly expressed gratitude for the opportunity to help someone like this young man.

Special Groups

Principal Baruti Kafele (bonus episode https://transformativeprincipal. org/baruti-kafele) is known for his young men empowerment groups. He helps young men and young women learn how to be men and women. This incredibly powerful weekly or monthly meeting encourages relationships and builds community. Because he is black, he specifically created this to teach young black men how to be men. But women, and specifically white women, want to help also but feel inadequate because they aren't like the students they're trying to help. This is a major fallacy in our efforts. We think that we need to be special or like our students to help them.

We don't.

We need to care.

When people ask Baruti this, he responds, "The question comes up all the time and it particularly comes up from women, white women who say, 'I respect everything you said, but look at you and look at me. Can I experience the same success?' And I always say to them, absolutely, because that boy, that young man is not necessarily looking at me or given me credit because I'm a black male nor discrediting you because you're a white woman. He wants to know if you're in his corner. He wants to know if you care. He wants to know if you're willing to do the things that you have to do to put you in position to meet him where he is. When we bring that level of commitment, dedication to him, that we're going to be just as successful as that black male that may look like that kid because of how bad we want it."

Jevon McCormick could have used anyone in his corner! All of our kids can use any of us in their corner.

Kids need to know we care about them. Kids need to know we are in their corner.

One person who took Baruti's suggestion of starting a young men's empowerment group is Jeff Carrus (episode 434). He is a principal in Katy, Texas, and not only started a young men's group, but he also started a rugby team in his school. Rugby in middle school can be a pretty scary thought, but how cool to give these young men an opportunity to do something really hard, like play rugby.

Jeff gathered some young men together and once a month has breakfast with them. He builds relationships in the community also by soliciting breakfast donations for this group, and by inviting guest speakers to come in and speak to the boys. The speakers come in and share how they've overcome adversity, and how they've gotten to where they are now.

But what I love about Jeff's story is that he didn't just copy what Baruti or someone else did. In fact, he didn't even learn it from Baruti. He learned it from someone in Dallas. Jeff said, "He had a young men's group and they did different service projects. He did it a little bit differently, but then I thought, you know, how can I do that? Because whenever we hear great things, we don't try to emulate it exactly as they do it. It's just not who we are. So, I try to find out what I am passionate about. How can I take this idea? And how's it going to benefit our kids? Because you know, it really it's about our population of students" and then they adapted it over the years to meet the needs of their students.

And this is key: Don't copy, build your own thing (Rob Carroll, episode 103).

Community Relationships

Building relationships goes beyond just your immediate school community (e.g., teachers, students, staff). It also includes building relationships with the community. Jeff did that especially well. So does Rob Carroll, former principal at South Heights Elementary. I think I could write a whole book about him. One of the ideas I stole from him was to visit the home of every student and make sure they knew that I cared about them. Man, that was awesome. Rob taught me that.

Rob's relationships run deep. He was principal at South Heights for more than 20 years. Over that time, he created a shopping extravaganza for his students at Christmas. He admits that a lot of schools are scared to celebrate holidays, but if you do it right, it can be a wonderful blending of traditions. The idea is to be inclusive. For his Christmas celebration, it starts with going to see a movie in the theater. Many of his students haven't ever seen a movie, and this is a special way for them to experience that.

The next stage is where his custodian and his team transform the gym into a winter wonderland and toy store, filled to the brim with donated gifts that the kids can buy with their school's currency, Blazer bucks.

The third stage is a parade through the community, complete with marching bands, floats, fire engine and police car. Rob said, "It's just a beautiful, beautiful thing. And we have parents and community members align the roads. Another cool thing is we have some of our elderly, they can't make it to the big city parade, that are always looking out their windows because they can see our parade. And this year our exciting thing that we're having is we're asking all of our former students that are currently in college to dress in their college sweatshirt, and they will walk together as a group."

College is really important to Rob, and he arranged for every grade level to take a field trip to a college or university every year. So, a student who has been at South Heights from kindergarten to sixth grade will have seen seven different college options! And they see them in person, in real life, not a virtual field trip.

We haven't even talked about all the other things that Rob does to build relationships with the community. Rob is the first to admit that this didn't all start in a day and that it took years. But once you have a plan and system in place, it gets easier to make it happen the next year. He believes that you should go big or go home. And that's pretty obvious from all that he did with his community.

If you follow Rob on Instagram (@1199Rob), you will see that his feed is full of pictures he takes with the people who make the magic happen at his school and in his community. I think I could probably write a whole book about all the great things Rob has done, but I'll let him write his own autobiography.

Chapter Summary

Relationships that involve care, candor, and conflict are completely essential for someone to be a transformative principal.

We build relationships so that we can have care, candor, and conflict that all deepen our experiences, commitment, and achievement.

When people are in crisis, they don't think about relationships, but they are still key. Sometimes, they even act as bullies themselves.

You can overcome challenges in relationships by assuming positive intent, having integrity, and being visible.

A long term strategy is to show your gratitude often as that helps build relationships.

Make people feel special in your school and in the community.

Key Questions

1. Are there negative relationships that you need to improve in your life? Where can you start with that?
2. Do you have care, concern, and conflict in your relationships?
3. What groups of kids can you focus on and make something special for them?
4. How can you invite your community to come into your school and build better relationships?
5. Who on your staff struggles in their relationships? How can you help them?

References

Lubelfeld, M., Polyak, N., & Caposey, P. J. (2021). *The unfinished leader: A school leadership framework for growth and development.* AASA Post Copub.

Pierson, R. (2013). *TED Talk: Every kid needs a champion.* https://www.youtube.com/watch?v=SFnMTHhKdkw

CHAPTER EIGHT
Hiring

Which is another lesson to be taken from his hiring: Surround yourself with people who are good in addition to being good at what they do.

Bob Iger

But these days, those who recruit and hire for companies, for instance, report that more than any time in memory the new generation of prospective employees shun working for places whose activities conflict with their personal values.

Daniel Goleman

Chapter Takeaway: Transformative principals recognize that hiring is a year-round process that transformative principals are always engaged in.

Reports of teacher shortages have been a constant backdrop in the United States for several years now. Transformative principals typically don't have a problem finding new staff for all the reasons we've spoken about in this book. If you have a Vital Vision, communicate effectively, build positive relationships, and support your teachers, you'll find that there is an endless list of people who want to be part of your school. It's a natural byproduct of the things we have been talking about. You can have that, too.

Hiring the best people for your school is vital. Todd Whitaker says that hiring may be the most important thing a principal does: "You can get a teacher more on board in 5 minutes in your interview than 5 years in your building." It behooves us as principals to ask the best questions we can to find out if someone will be a good fit for our school. As Bill Daggett says, "Culture trumps strategy. Every. Single. Time." When interviewing, you must find the best person you can. It is even acceptable to wait as long as you need to until you find that person. Sometimes, a person serving as a long term sub is better than a poor teacher. If you have ever hired the wrong person for a job, you know that is true. Just preparing to hire teachers is a multi-step process.

Hiring is a year-round job, one that takes on different aspects at different times in the year.

Hiring can be risky. Or rather, I should say, hiring is RISCHI (pronounced risky).

The stages to hiring great people are RISCHI:

Recruit
Screen
Interview
Cultural fit
Hire
Introduce

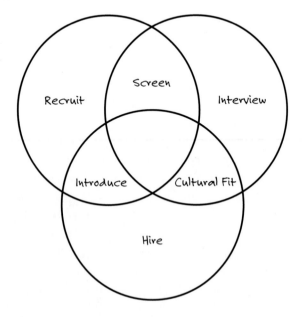

I like to see this as a three-circle Venn diagram because there is overlap in the areas. We'll dive into each of these areas shortly. It is also effective to think of this as a never-ending circle! Where you are regularly doing each of these activities.

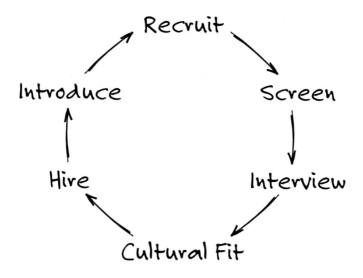

With teacher shortages that have plagued our industry for years being exacerbated by the pandemic, more than ever we need to take a serious step in hiring people effectively. A recent study by the Learning Policy Institute called "A Coming Crisis in Teaching: Teaching Supply, Demand, and Shortages in the U.S.," shows that in 2021 the demand for new teachers would be 300,000 and the amount of teachers available would be less than 200,000. That's a projected shortage of 100,000 teachers! And that was in 2016, before the pandemic was even a thing. In 2021, we've had governments requesting retired teachers come back to take the load off of other teachers. Districts are offering signing bonuses and trying to attract teachers. While those may be nice, that's nothing compared to you implementing what you read in this book! Being a transformative principal is how we solve our teacher shortage. And I'm going to show you how to do recruit and hire amazing teachers.

I've worked hard to include actionable advice for you here to make sure you can attract the top talent to your school and that they will want to stay there forever! But remember, they will come for the job but they will stay for the Vital Vision.

Before we go any further, imagine for a moment what hiring process could look like in five years. In five years, you have very low turnover. It happens, but people want to stay at your school because it is such a great place. When there is turnover, and opportunities for new staff to come on board, you first make sure all your current people are in the correct places. Then, you get to take your pick from the people who you already know will be great at your school and invite them to join you. You have the perfect placement for them, and they already have friends at your school so you know they will be a good fit. Just imagine how powerful that would be for everyone. It's possible, and that's how transformative principals hire new staff.

This isn't just an ideal situation, either. It's possible! Melinda Miller (episode 11) said, "So there were some teachers that were hired that summer by who was here before me, and then I started hiring 10 years ago. If I didn't want them here, they wouldn't be here." People don't stick around when they don't like the environment or the direction the school is heading, and once you hire someone, they are your person. They are committed to you and the vision that you had for the school when you brought them on.

Recruit

First, we'll start with recruitment. You are always recruiting for your school. Anywhere, anytime, you should constantly be looking out for and inviting the best people you can find to join your school. If you wait to recruit until it is hiring season, you've already missed the boat!

You can't put the people in the right seats on the bus until you have gotten them on the bus in the first place. When you find the right person, you want them on the bus with you as soon as possible, and then work hard to get them to the right seat as fast as possible. I hired a guy named Farrel in my school in Fairbanks. I didn't care what his job title was, I just wanted him working with my kids. He was an interventionist, a special ed aide, an afterschool coordinator, and a basketball coach. I just needed that amazing positive male role model around my students. Once I met him, I started trying to get him into our school in any capacity possible.

Hiring great people to work with our kids is the most important thing we can do. Think for a moment about all the grief and pain that could be saved if that awful teacher had never been hired. Think also for a moment if you could double the number of really dedicated and effective teachers that you have in your school. The impact on your students and communities would be completely changed. Doug Hallenbeck taught me this all the way back in episode 8. He said, "If you do your due diligence before they walk in the door, you are going to save yourself thousands of hours of time!" And this is the truth. And that's why we start with recruiting. We want to find the best people for our school.

If you've done a vital vision for your school, you will attract the kind of people that want to work with you.

Ryan Moran, on his own podcast, shares an example of Tom Bilyeu, founder of Quest Nutrition. Their vision was "to end metabolic disease. That was their guiding principle. The way that they did that was creating delicious high protein food that easily replaces junk food." (Moran 2021). When people were clear on that vision, it made it so much easier to find the people, strategies, and products that would fulfill that vision. The same can be true for your school. *AJ Stich* (episode 391) is the founding principal of The Dayton School. Their vision is to help kids be successful adults by staying in touch with them until and helping them succeed until the students are at least 27! He says, "We're currently hiring our founding cohort of teachers and we've had these discussions in great depth because we know, and I assume people that are listening to this are going to know that it just, it starts and ends with teachers. We're looking for, the Navy Seal of teachers, but to your point, they need to have flexibility of mind because the traditional school model, where, you have 20 to 30 kids in your class and you deliver a mini lesson to all of them and you give a worksheet or even on the more progressive side you give a project or a rubric that kids, you know, self-assess, and then they do an exit ticket. At the end. You did that sort of factory model of schooling."

Because AJ has such a clear vision, someone who isn't interested in that idea of working with kids until they're 27 is not going to want to work at his school. But that clear vision is a big part of why someone would want to work at his school.

The other reason we should be recruiting all the time is because there is a real value in having a high quality teacher in your building. AJ continues, "I mean, having the right people in front of the kids, there's a dollar value to it. You look at some of the research out there and having a teacher that's one standard deviation above the mean is worth $40,000. Every year a kid has that quality of teacher."

Imagine posting a position and wading through dozens of resumes, but actually already knowing and understanding why those people want to come with you! Contrast that with my regular experience in Alaska of looking at a list of applicants, whose resumes all look essentially the same, with no indication of whether they'd be a good fit.

A fellow Alaskan principal, Clare Fulp (episode 174) had a similar issue, excepting she was running a summer school program specifically for refugees around Anchorage, Alaska. She really needed to be recruiting from anywhere she could to find the right kind of people for that work. She says, "I was really looking for the passion for kids and a great attitude, because I think you would probably agree that can take anybody so far. And that great attitude piece is so key for summertime work because if you don't do a good job and if it's not fun, the kids just won't come."

Kids won't want to come if their teachers don't have good attitudes. Clare needs to recruit throughout the year to find people who can hand that kind of summertime work because otherwise, kids don't show, and there's evidence of their waning interest. Clare continues, "This isn't a mandatory thing. This is they all get on the bus and they all come. And we had a couple of classes last year where every day I'd notice the attendance would get a little lower. The classes where the attendance was really high [were the classes] they were doing really high engagement things."

She concludes, "we do ourselves a great disservice when we don't make that the intention of what we're hiring for." And that hiring process starts much earlier than the job posting.

It starts with recruitment. You may know someone for five years before they are ready to join your school. Those five years of communication, sharing ideas, and collaborating will not be wasted.

If you have great staff members inviting their friends to come to work, this is the best-case scenario. New hires will know what's expected, have a friend and mentor built in, and will know more of what to expect that is unique to your school.

Encourage and invite your staff to invite their friends to your recruiting list.

Hiring doesn't start when you post your first job. As Dr. TJ Vari and Dr. Joe Jones (episode 451) said, "Hiring and recruitment is a year-round job, where different activities are emphasized at different times of the year." They emphasize retention in their book, *Retention for a Change* (Jones et al., 2021), but in addition to retaining the teachers you have, you also have to make a plan to recruit great teachers to your school. This includes a piece Joe said is really important, "building relationships with institutions of higher education so you can get student teachers."

Action Step: Create a list of potential hires!

This may sound like overkill, but I would start today cultivating a list of email addresses of people you want to recruit to your school. Then, once a quarter I would write a letter talking about the great things that are happening at your school and send it to those people. Don't be shy about stating the purpose of the newsletter. It's to let people know what's going on in your school because they might want a job there someday.

Screen

As you're recruiting, you should be screening for people who are and are not a good fit for your school. You're not going to be able to hire the right people if you don't have a vision for where you are going. Your vision is what attracts and screens people to see if they should be in your school. Do you sense a recurring theme?

All throughout your recruiting, you need to be screening the people who are interested. If you're recruiting long term, this should be easy. You can become friendly with potential candidates and start giving advice early on how to make their careers great. And screen out people who won't work well.

When people send you resumes or apply for your teaching positions, I learned an idea from Rick Wormeli where he suggests that you write a 1-page letter that clearly outlines your expectations at the school. I've included a sample of my letter for you below. Feel free to use it to help you improve your processes to get the best people in your pool.

This letter should positively state the important initiatives and efforts you engage in at your school. Be sure to end the letter with something like, "If this letter excites you, please call me to schedule an interview. If this letter makes you feel like you would not like to work here, that is fine, too. We wish you the best of luck."

After a job is posted and you have applicants, call each person individually and personally. Schedule interviews at a time that works for the candidate. Jimmy Casas says that you want to show them that you will be flexible from the beginning. If they apply for a job at your school, and they could be a good fit, you want them to be a superstar, and making the whole hiring process good for them will help the settle in to your school and buy in to your plans and initiatives.

In Episode 135, I talked with Rachel Yanof and she has a clear screening process to help know who she should hire. She says, "First question: you either believe in this mission or you don't and if you don't wonderful power to you, but it's not going to work here. So when you're hiring people, the first question is, do you believe all kids can go to college? And are you willing to make that happen? If the answer is anything other than absolutely. When can I start, then that's not a good fit for your school." Her screening process is very focused because her school's very clear vision is that all kids go to college. Anything other than that is just not going to work.

In episode 16, Fidel Montero, principal of a diverse high school talked about the importance of screening based on previous experience. "Making sure that you're hiring the right person when you're going through that process. And I think hopefully you have a way of identifying the right fit of candidates to work in a title one school, to work in a school that's highly impacted socioeconomically or who has a high number of students of color." You want to see if people have shown success in working with the kind of students that are at your school. One teacher made it through our screening process and came in for the interview. I could tell she just wanted a job teaching to "get her foot in the door." I asked her specifically about that, and she agreed, that's what she was interested in. I then described my school, and she said she didn't think she would like it there. It didn't sound like fun to her. So, before we started interviewing, she was out the door, with my blessing and permission.

In order to have a school like the Dayton School, you have to be willing to do things differently. AJ Stich talks about screening for a mindset, "That's a big factor in what we're hiring, but also just that flexibility of mind to do things differently and say, 'Hey, you know what? Whatever I've done, whether it's a traditional or progressive model of schooling, I've had success. But I also recognize that there's other ways to educate that are as good and maybe better than what I've been doing.'" If AJ isn't hearing or seeing evidence of that mindset, he knows it's not going to work in his school.

So regardless of what you are screening for, you need to have criteria that makes sense for your school. Don't just adopt the criteria of someone else, develop your own criteria and make sure you're clear about what will and won't make someone successful in your school.

Action Step: Write your letter

I've included my letter that I actually sent to candidates. Those who called me right after reading almost always got the job. Write your letter today. When someone applies for a job, send them your letter. If it speaks to them, they'll want to be part of your school.

Dear [Name],

Thank you so much for applying to inspire students at our school. If you are the successful candidate, you will love teaching here. The scenery is beautiful, the children amazing, and the staff very supportive and eager to help each of our students be successful.

There are three things I want you to be aware of before we start the interview process.

First, our students are our focus. We make decisions based on what is best for them. Sometimes, this means that we don't do things like other schools. For example, we utilize trauma-informed practices to make sure that our students know that we respect the place where they are, and are willing to help them get better themselves.

Second, Professional Development for teachers is how we make sure they meet the first goal. It is our responsibility is to be in charge of our own professional development. At our school, we are constantly improving ourselves through our own research, participation in online opportunities, recording our own lessons, attending district inservice, furthering our own education by taking classes at the college level, reading books, and pretty much anything else that helps us improve. We believe that we can all improve, and we constantly seek feedback to help us find where we can get better. We use a personalized PD approach, which means that PD sessions are scheduled in advance, and teachers can either attend those sessions or do their own PD at their level sometime during that week. For example, if we are doing PD on standards-based grading, we will have a session and teachers who engaged in their own PD during that week in their own time would be exempt from the meeting. We make sure that requirements and big ideas are communicated clearly so we can all be on the same page.

Finally, open communication empowers us to accomplish the first two goals. We can't help kids if we don't communicate openly with everyone. We can't ensure that we implement effective professional development if we don't communicate openly about our weaknesses, strengths and needs. On my door, I have communication cards, which help set the stage for communication. These are sentence starters for things that are hard to talk with your boss about. I get that. We have to communicate openly for us to be the best.

These three core values help us get where we want to be. We value continuous improvement, and we know that we need to work with each other to reach our goals.

If this letter excites you, please call me to schedule an interview (801) 753-8476. If this letter makes you feel like you would not like to work here, that is fine, too. We wish you the best of luck!

Thanks,

Jethro

Interview

After you screen them, you'll want to interview them. And interviewing is more than just sitting down and asking questions. There's a whole process just around interviewing that we will dive into a bit deeper here.

The interview process can be daunting for both sides, and again, if you already know the people, it makes this part much easier. Imagine sitting down for an interview just to fine tune some perspectives that need a little bit more examination, rather than just getting to know someone for the first time!

How many times have people been hired as teachers after just one interview, no teaching opportunities, and no further discovery? How can you really know if they'll work?

A seasoned leader once told me to always trust your gut, because if you ever have a feeling someone isn't going to work out, you're probably going to be proven right. But that doesn't always mean your gut saying yes is the right choice!

Before the Interview

The interview starts way before the interview. How people react, respond, pay attention, and everything helps inform you of the kind of person they'll be at your school. You're also auditioning for them, and the way you treat them shows something as well. You are communicating your values and your vision from the very beginning, so be true to your values and who you are from the beginning.

Are you flexible? Then set up interview times when it is convenient for them.

Are you strict and traditional? Then share that in everything you do.

The Right Answers

For the questions you decide to use, you need to also take time to define what a great answer to your questions looks like. First, you need to define what great answers are yourself. Then, you need to work with your team to determine what the team feels are the "right" answers. When you and your interview team are on the same page, you will know which candidate will be successful sooner.

Interview questions need to get at things that matter. It's not always about the answer someone gives.

Mike Rogers (episode 42), a principal in St. Paul, Minnesota seeks to learn if someone will be great in the classroom in the interview. He say, "Are they going to be willing to try new things, or that really bring an energy to the classroom? And this is something that I think I'm fairly good at picking up in the course of an interview when first talking to a teacher. And then one of the questions I like to ask when I interview teachers is what is it about this particular [age] group of students?" This is a question that reveals what the person thinks about a particular age group. As a middle school teacher, I could always tell when I was talking to another educator who got middle school. You either love them or hate them. I had one teacher who wanted nothing to do with middle schoolers, and it showed every day. She was a transfer to our school and it was not a good fit. Getting her back into a high school was a blessing for everyone!

As you ask questions, take the time to determine what is a good answer.

Interview Team

Rob Carroll (episode 104) has students on the interviewing team. "Well, they loved it. They really felt empowered that day. I kind of bragged about it the following year, they were like, 'Hey, you know, we helped hire that one right there. Yep. We picked her out. She was pretty good.' And you know, as far as the applicants when they would walk in, if they were all taken aback and they couldn't handle being interviewed by a group of kids that really thrown that much, I would really question their ability to lead a bunch of students."

Who you have on the interview team matters. Again, if you're following what I'm suggesting, the candidates will already have friends at the school and that will help them feel comfortable through the whole interview process. Rob added, "You could tell the ones, some of those teachers we hired through that process, they've been right on. And when they walked in the difference, the teacher that facilitated that, the difference you saw was those teachers that we ended up hiring their eyes just lit up. When they saw the students are going to interview, they just went into this whole other level of excitement."

Rob sees this as a filter to help him know which teachers are going to be great. "So for me, what a great filter, what a great first test to let you know that you're an, a student driven student advocate school. We're not messing around. This is what we're about."

Interview Process

The most important thing is finding out if someone will add value to your school. There are lots of opinions and processes about everything that needs to happen, but that is goal number one: get the right person. However you need to find that right person is the right thing to do. And once you have that right person, you don't need to do any more.

Surely, your district will have processes that you need to follow, and do follow them, but also feel confident in your ability to hire someone effectively.

Most principals would agree interviews at a minimum should consist of at least one interview with a hiring team, and it would be good to include teaching interviews. Having been a principal in Alaska, this is tough to make happen but it is possible. Sometimes, those things need to happen over video and sometimes they need to be in person.

I've heard some principals say they want to ask all the questions, and do all the interviews. Others want to delegate that to others. Again, it doesn't matter too much. Transformative principals do enough to ensure they have the right person, and they get to define how much is "enough". For example, Colin Andrews, principal of a school in New Zealand likes to have everyone else ask the questions as he sits silently taking notes. In episode 41, he says, "I'll start the interview off and I'll just sit and watch and I'll make notes. So, I let the other three do all the questioning and I've developed techniques and it's good practice that my Deputy Principals ask the questions and I reflect."

I asked him what he was looking for specifically and he said body language, a deep thought how they answer the question, but then he shared a great story. He added, "Their enthusiasm for life. I had one teacher who came in and sat down and she had just completed a law degree. Then she'd done a postgraduate diploma in teaching and she sat down and said, 'Colin, I just want to teach. I just love teaching.' So I virtually stopped the interview there. We offered her a job amazingly."

When you know you have the right person, move on to the next stage. At that point, the interview is over.

Action Step: Define great answers

Take the interview questions you already have and draft *answers* that are off the charts awesome, and share them with the hiring committee. People should know what the "right answers" are. But it's not always exactly what they say, but how they say it and what the underlying tone is.

If you don't have great questions, you can get some here: http://www.transformativeprincipal.org/hiring/ I crowd-sourced some great questions from my friends on social media and include them in this download.

Culture Fit

The cultural fit overlaps with hiring and interviewing, because you can't always judge that in the interview. This is where references come in. I don't list checking references as one of the things you should because references are incredibly subjective. The whole hiring process is, and many people put a lot of emphasis on references. But that doesn't tell the whole story. But there are aspects that you can figure out.

I had one teacher who was inappropriate in her emotional relationships with students. Nothing worthy of losing her license, but inappropriate for our situation. I told this to the next principal who interviewed her. He said, "I appreciate your concern, but she would be majorly shunned by the faculty if she acted that way here. I don't think it will be a problem at all." My answer to the age-old question of "would you hire her again?" was a resounding no, but because of the culture at his school, he was not worried about it all.

You need to make sure that people will fit into the culture. Dave Ramsey has said that he takes his potential hires out to dinner with his spouse and their spouse, and if there are any red flags, they don't proceed yet.

You don't have to go to that extreme, but you do want to know that they will be a good fit. Tours of the school, informal conversations, and anything else you can do to get to know them and have them know your school is going to be a step in the right direction.

In another situation, a principal related this story, "I said that I thought I was hiring someone to be a team player. She was not showing me that. She took the discussion to a larger discussion of what we do as a nation with education. She said she wants to do what is best for kids. I told her I do too. The problem with that argument is that she and I can both make clear, valid arguments about how what we want is best for kids. It's pointless. I told her I need a team player who is joining in our work, not fighting against it." This principal's cultural fit was someone who was willing to join the work, not fight against it.

I once had a teacher apply for a position, and she just wanted a job. She was a sweet young woman, but in the interview she talked about how much she loved spending time with her family and how they did stuff together all the time. I had to level with her in the interview, "You need to understand that we live on an island, in the Gulf of Alaska. It's an all-day flight back to your family, and at least a five-day drive, plus the 11-hour ferry ride. This isn't going to work out." She replied that she really needed a job and felt confident that she could do the work. I assured her that I believed she could do the work but that she would never be happy living on an island so far away from her family.

Eric Sheninger (episode 12) noted the importance of hiring, "Even some of the veteran teachers, 30-plus years, are leading the charge in their own way. I think it's all about hiring the person with the right mindset. Someone that wants to learn someone that's not afraid to take risks. Someone who will adapt, collaborate model, continuously learn. Those are the things I look for relating to experience. I could care less if you are the right fit for the students of New Milford. Will you fit in to this culture that we're continuously revamping to provide a better learning experience for our students?"

James Briscoe (episode 34) was a superintendent in Chicago and then Sandy, Utah. He said a good way to see if someone is a cultural fit is to ask how they would implement something. He says, "There's a difference between having a vision and having the ability to articulate. It's really critical when you become a leader, anyone can share a fish, but can you explain to me exactly how you're going to implement that vision? I would look for people when they interview to tell me how they're going to implement what they believe needs to happen within that organization or school building in, in really doing the homework and understand the culture and how to move it forward."

Know What You Can Tolerate When Checking References

There's not a perfect teacher out there. You'll always have to settle. Know what you can tolerate when you're checking references so that you can have the peace of mind of knowing what you've gotten yourself into. By way of example, I once hired a special education teacher whose previous supervisor told me she wasn't great about paperwork but was really great with the kids. The kids adored her and the parents really appreciated her, but the principal was happy to see her go because he had to constantly follow up on her paperwork. I inquired further about what she wasn't great at: deadlines, sending paperwork home, getting signatures in individualized education program (IEP) meetings, and providing progress reports on time. I asked her directly about all this and realized she wasn't a paperwork person and was always going to struggle. Luckily for her and for me, we had a position in our district called the Special Ed Clerk, which took care of almost all of that work. I agreed that I or the assistant principal would always ensure that signatures were taken at the IEP meeting, and that took care of that. Paperwork is important, but it's not as important as the kids. She was on a team with another special education teacher who cared more about the paperwork than the kids. They were able to teach each other something.

Action Step: Define fit

Take a moment and look at your best teachers. What do they do and say that makes you recognize they are the best? Then write a short list of those things and make a list of questions you would ask references, the candidate, and others to see if this teacher really will be a good fit.

Hire Them

There's a whole process around hiring someone. Many principals unwisely turn this responsibility over to the human resources department. One of my favorite things to say to new hires is, "We are in a bureaucratic system. It moves slowly and then all of a sudden very quickly. I'm here to help you get everything taken care of that you need to join us at our school. So, stay in touch."

This seemingly simple step is often overlooked by many. To be "chosen" is one of the best feelings in the world. Make it special for that person. Make sure they know how important your job of hiring is and how impactful their day-to-day work will be.

Don't offer the job and never talk to them until the first day of school. Give them opportunities to be involved in the school before they start working there officially.

My friend Brad Gustafson always introduces his new teachers in a creative YouTube video. In the 2016-2017 school year, he did a Jedi-themed introduction and said all the new teachers scored higher than Luke Skywalker. Watch this introduction here: https://www.youtube.com/watch?v=jZO-TnPER4o

How do you think that makes his teachers feel when they get hired? It makes them feel special. Transformative principals take advantage of this opportunity to make the hiring process an exciting and affirming time.

The other part of hiring that is important is getting people in the right places. I mentioned how I hired Farrell and I just wanted someone like him in my building and would use him however I could. Frank Schofield is the superintendent in Logan School District. In episode 54, he says, "If you've read *Good to Great* by Jim Collins (2001), a big point is first one is to get the right people on the bus. And we focus on that a lot with our hiring, which is good, but it's just as essential with your team and you try to create a team and say, 'Well, we're going to take the most senior person at each grade level, or we're going to have one person from each department. And that's your only criteria for identifying your team members?' You're going to run the risk of having a really poorly functioning team, but if you get the right people on the bus with your leadership teams, you can do amazing, amazing things."

No only should you hire the right people, but you should also put them in the right place.

Finally, not everyone you interview is going to be the best right now. They may have potential in the future. If that superintendent built a relationship even though I wasn't the right candidate, I'd be open to talking with him because he showed me who he was before.

Action Step: Offer the job

Establish a process for how you're going to extend job invitations and how you're going to let people know they weren't the right candidate today. Keep the conversation open if they might be a good fit in the future.

Introduce

Finally, introduce leads into more recruiting. You want your star teachers to introduce you to their friends who are also star teachers. This is an ongoing cycle that pretty much never ends and lasts all year.

You want your current staff members to be the main source of your recruiting efforts. People love working with their friends, and if you can get their friends to join you and them, it's going to be even better.

Tom Hierck (episode 188): You know, I can give you our purpose in the hiring process. Go back to the hiring process. You just did. I will take 10 minutes during the interview and slide across our purpose to you and say, "Hey, Jethro, knowing the skills you have, how do you see that aligning with what we believe to be our purpose here at XYZ school?"

[00:06:28] *James Briscoe:* What's your process? I think that's critical. It's a big difference there when people are interviewing is to try to dig, like, how are you actually going to do things. Tell me some things you've got.

From the moment you decide to hire them to their 90th day is all part of the hiring process. It includes onboarding and making sure they know what is going on. I suggest creating a series of emails that you can send them explaining how things work in your school so they are prepared. Then, when they are on staff, ensure they have a mentor and make sure that you stay in regular touch with them.

In episode 24, William Parker talks about the importance of sharing your values with your staff so they can know who they should be looking to recruit as well. He says, "We communicate a lot about vision and in those conversations, when we're doing hirings about the priorities that we have of hiring teachers who are both great instructors and also compassionate. That's been a running theme here for a long time at our school that my former principal established and we've continued."

I mentioned onboarding in the chapter about relationships, and I'll briefly address it here as well. Onboarding new teachers can save you a lot of time and many headaches. It can even get you out of a situation where you've hired the wrong person, but didn't know it. This happened to me. After getting the emails I sent out the person wrote me an email and said, "I'm glad you let me know what life at your school is going to be like. Now that I understand better, I don't think I'm ready to move to an island in the Gulf of Alaska yet!" It was good for both of us she didn't come.

What is essential in onboarding? That of course depends on your school and what matters most to you, but if you've been paying attention, it's most likely your Vital Vision and the Culture.

Spend your time and energy reminding and cultivating those two areas.

Action Step: Establish your onboarding plan

What are the five or six things people have to know to be successful at your school? Create a way to deliver that to them before they start working.

Four Mistakes

Hiring is the most important job that we do. Who we hire matters not only to the person we are hiring and their students, but also to the rest of the team at the school. You have surely seen how a toxic hire can poison the well for so many other people in your school.

In order to get better teachers, we need to not make three simple mistakes that almost every principal has learned their lesson on:

Warm body

Sometimes, we just need a warm body to be in our school. But it is almost never worth it to hire someone just to have someone. Even though it is hard, wait until you have the right person for the job.

Good X does not mean good teacher

Some people are really great at being substitutes, but not all. One principal shared with me that she had a substitute teacher who was just a dynamic, awesome sub, every time she showed up. She thought that person would make an excellent teacher, but when it came down to creating her own ideas and plans, she really failed to measure up. It was a hard lesson to learn.

Whatever someone might be good at, it doesn't always mean they will be a good teacher. Sometimes people can blossom in one area and completely fail in another. That doesn't mean don't offer your substitute teachers jobs, but it does mean that you can't assume.

Too good to be true

Multiple principals have the seemingly best candidate in the world walk into their schools and they think they are saved. They get enamored with the shiny references or information from the other person, but that's sometimes too good to be true. This is only a problem when you don't take the time to do all the other processes related to hiring. You still have to make sure the cultural fit is there.

Too fast

Sometimes we hire people too fast. We don't do enough due diligence. We need to follow the RISCHI model to help us find the right people. Take the time that is needed, but no more. Go slow to go fast.

If you follow the RISCHI model for hiring, you won't make these mistakes.

Chapter Summary

Hiring is the most important job you have. Do it well, and you'll reap great rewards. Do it poorly, and you could spend inordinate hours cleaning up your mess.

Use the RISCHI acronym to make better hiring processes and decisions.

Recruit—always be recruiting.

Screen—screen people for cultural fit throughout the process.

Interview—the interview process is important, and tells one part of their story.

Cultural fit—examine how they will fit in to your culture.

Hire them—make the offer, and make it exciting for them.

Introduce—introduce them to your school, and get them to start recruiting for your school, too.

Don't make the mistakes.

Key Questions

1. Has your hiring process resulted in the kind of teachers you want to hire?
2. What areas of the RISCHI model would benefit from closer examination?
3. Who are your best teachers? What would you do if you could get more like them? Are you actively searching for those teachers?
4. What besides references can tell you how a person will fit into your school?
5. When do you "know" a person is a fit? What does that look like to you?

References

Collins, J. (2001). Good to great: Why some companies make the leap and others don't. Harper Business.

Jones, J., Thomas-El, S., & Vari, T. J. (2021). Retention for a change: Motivate, inspire, and energize your school culture. Rowman & Littlefield.

Iger, R. (2019). *The ride of a lifetime: Lessons learned from 15 years as CEO of the Walt Disney Company* (First edition). Random House/Penguin Random House LLC.

Sutcher, L., Darling-Hammond, L., & Carver-Thomas, D. (2016, September 15). *A Coming Crisis in Teaching? Teacher Supply, Demand, and Shortages in the U.S.* https://learningpolicyinstitute.org/product/coming-crisis-teaching

Capitalism.com Zero (n.d.) *To $1M In 12 Months—For 2022 And Beyond.* Retrieved December 29, 2021, from https://www.capitalism.com/podcast/12months-2022/

CHAPTER NINE
Culture

If we are to preserve culture we must continue to create it.

Johan Huizinga

Culture is a way of coping with the world by defining it in detail.

Malcolm Bradbury

If you want to change the culture, you will have to start by changing the organization.

Mary Douglas

Whoever controls the media, the images, controls the culture.

Allen Ginsberg

The moment you give up your principles, and your values, you are dead, your culture is dead, your civilization is dead. Period.

Oriana Fallaci

Education must, be not only a transmission of culture but also a provider of alternative views of the world and a strengthener of the will to explore them.

Jerome Bruner

Culture is the air we breathe all around us.

Josh Fox

Culture makes people understand each other better. And if they understand each other better in their soul, it is easier to overcome the economic and political barriers. But first they have to understand that their neighbour is, in the end, just like them, with the same problems, the same questions.

Paulo Coelho

We live in a culture where everyone's opinion, view, and assessment of situations and people spill across social media, a lot of it anonymously, much of it shaped by mindless meanness and ignorance.

Mike Barnicle

Culture hides much more than it reveals, and strangely enough, what it hides, it hides most effectively from its own participants.

Edward T. Hall

Chapter Takeaway: Transformative principals do all the other things that make up culture, so when it is time to focus on culture, it's visible and present.

Every child deserves to have a transformative principal. When all the things I've discussed in this book are done to the best of your ability, you're going to have something that you really wish were tangible and easy to define: Culture. The birthplace of everything. Culture eats strategy for breakfast. Culture is the big domino. Culture is the foundation of everything in a school. Culture permeates everything else that we do. In fact, if I were to write a book about school *anything*, and didn't address culture in some way, nobody would ever read it.

On the Transformative Principal podcast, I've interviewed a lot of leaders. Every single one of them has great ideas and strategies that they are implementing in their work. At the time of this writing, 25 percent of my published podcast episodes have talked about culture. It's obviously a huge topic, and mane people are commenting on it. From Jason Glass talking about culture in a district of 80,000 students in Colorado to Clare Fulp talking about culture as principal of a refugee school in Alaska, they all have the same message: Culture trumps everything. As I've listened to each leader speak, I've learned that there is some aspect of truth in what they say, even when looking at it with several different lenses.

But there's a dirty little secret here. The more you focus on culture, the less it will improve. Culture is the makeup of everything else.

As I recounted in the introduction, one principal came to me asking for help improving her school's culture. I asked her how she was taking care of herself and she laughed, saying "not very well." I told her if she wanted to fix her school's culture, she needed to take care of herself. She didn't understand what I was saying, but in less than 12 months, following what we talk about in this book, she was already seeing the difference in her school's culture without spending any time "fixing it."

She complained that culture in her school would suffer as soon as she started focusing on instruction. She knew she needed to have high expectations for instruction, but she felt that she couldn't because then culture would suffer. I've seen plenty of schools that have high expectations for instruction and have great cultures. We went back to her self-care, and I invited her to start there.

As she continued working on herself, recognizing her inability to control others, and started giving teachers the support they needed, the culture improved. It improved bit by bit at first, but then in big waves later on.

Culture is how we treat people every day. It's how people treat us. It's how clear our vision is. It's how well we communicate and build relationships. It's about showing gratitude. It's about hiring the right people. It's about everyone being on board with your chosen learning framework. It's about recognizing strengths and delegating effectively. It's about taking care of ourselves.

Culture is huge. It's the foundation of everything. Everything contributes to it. And, by extension, it's nearly impossible to focus solely on culture and make it better. Well, I guess it's not impossible, but it's not a good use of time.

Culture is like paint drying. You can watch it and monitor it, but the best way to deal with it is to do the work, then walk away and let it do its thing. Then, when the time is right, check back in and see if it is dry yet. Take care of your other business and the culture will take care of itself.

Healthy Organizations Have Great Culture

In education, we usually use the word *culture* to describe what Patrick Lencioni (2012) calls "a healthy organization" in his book, *The Advantage*. He's talking about the business world, but there are applications for our work here. He gives guidance on how to identify a healthy organization: "A good way to recognize health is to look for the signs that indicate an organization has it. These include minimal politics and confusion, high degrees of morale and productivity, and very low turnover among good employees" (2012, p. 5). These organizational health indicators do make a difference. I'm simplifying it to culture, even though Lencioni said that organizational health is "way more than culture" to make it easier for us to comprehend, and because that is the term we use in schools all the time. As you've seen throughout this book, so many things make up the culture in your school, or the organizational health of your school.

As educators, we are very smart! We've been through the K–12 school system, we've all received bachelor's degrees and master's degrees, and many have received doctorates. However, that doesn't mean that the organizations automatically have great cultures because we are in them. Lencioni said, "The seminal difference between successful companies and mediocre or unsuccessful ones has little, if anything, to do with what they know or how smart they are; it has everything to do with how healthy they are" (2012, p. 8).

Through this book, you've learned the ways to make your organization have a great culture. One chapter I just couldn't fit in was about instructional frameworks. I wrote 10,000 words about it, and in the end, it didn't make sense to include.

Why couldn't I fit it in? Because your instructional framework doesn't matter.

That may be hard for some people to hear as I lump personalized learning, standards-based instruction, professional learning communities (PLCs), International Baccalaureate (IB), and more all into one simple statement, but your instructional framework doesn't matter if you have a great culture!

This is a good illustration of what Lencioni calls smart versus healthy.

A smart school focuses on the instructional framework because it is easy, comfortable, and it's what they were trained in. A healthy school focuses on minimal politics and confusion, high morale, and low turnover. What does that mean? It means they are unified on an instructional framework regardless of what it is. If it's personalized learning, they're all in. If it's PLCs, they're all in. If it's IB, they're all in.

I once worked with a school where every teacher was given permission to teach however they wanted to, use whatever lesson plans they thought were best, and use completely different approaches for gifted and talented students. Each teacher had their own policy for homework, late work, attendance, and classroom behavior. A couple of years later, the principal saw that there were major struggles among her team. There was no consistency and there was a lot of confusion. Teachers sought the advanced classes because they had even more freedom, and new teachers were relegated to the unfortunate and classic "There's your textbook on that wall—good luck" as their orientation. Every year, new teachers came and went. Few stayed, partly due to enrollment issues, partly due to the isolated, heavy workload.

When I worked with them again, the principal had seen the dysfunction that was evident in their school. She recognized they were all smart people, but they were not a healthy organization. They did not have a great culture. She did many of the things in this book, and found silos in her school and a lack of unity. She worked with the teachers to find something that would bridge the chasms that had been built up between teachers, and they settled on the International Baccalaureate Middle Years Program. Many things changed very quickly, not because they chose IB but because they got healthy. Voices were heard, politics were (nearly) eliminated, confusion was gone, and they were ready to invest in such a way that few good teachers ever wanted to leave.

To the outside observer, it is easy to say that IB changed it all for them. Even some of the teachers believed that was the issue. IB was a smart strategy, but it took the principal's healthy approach to make it work. She said that it wasn't the IB program that made the difference, it was the work of the teachers to prepare for it that made the difference. Rather than every teacher operating in a silo, they needed to work together.

When they started to work together, they started to understand each other. She changed the culture. A new instructional framework was the natural result of changing the culture because people could see where they needed to improve. Had she not done the work on everything that makes up culture, the transition to IB would have been majorly flawed!

By contrast, I worked with another school district that took the idea that "if we just change our instructional model, it will fix all our other problems." Unfortunately, they did not focus on the culture of their district. They spent a considerable amount of money to implement an instructional framework, and because the groundwork was not done correctly, they never achieved a change in culture. They focused on the problem they had, no instructional framework, and thought that an instructional framework would make it better. Inside the district, politics were rampant. Once the superintendent was displeased with someone, that person was ostracized. The superintendent would have "golden ones" who were the teachers and principals whom she liked, and they were elevated above others. Principals and teachers would snipe at one another as soon as they showed some promise to prevent themselves from being emotionally demoted in the superintendent's eyes. One principal received the highest accolades one year, only to be yanked out of the school they led the following year, because the principal fell out of favor with the superintendent. Several other principals openly mocked the new instructional framework, stating that the district would "get an idea like this every few years, and they never last. We just wait them out and go back to how we've always done it." Staff were stressed and frustrated. Because the work was not done on all the other stuff you've learned in this book, the new instructional framework was destined to fail. And fail it did, despite considerable talent, money, infrastructure, and planning.

The contrast of these two approaches to change the instructional framework only deepens the need for us to focus on more than just one aspect of schooling when we seek to make change.

The first principal changed her school to have a great culture. She didn't just adopt a new instructional framework but did the work necessary to make it work. The school district had adopted a new instructional framework thinking that would make their other problems go away. It can't.

Culture Is the Big Domino

As I mentioned in the introduction, culture is the big domino. It is the one that, when it is good, it makes everything else easier. When it is toxic, it makes everything else nearly impossible.

But it's big, and it's hard to control by focusing just on culture alone. Bill Daggett said that culture eats strategy for breakfast. This quote, attributed to Peter Drucker, implies the need for our culture to be top notch at all times if we want to implement change that matters.

When we understand that culture eats strategy for breakfast, we understand why my example in the last session makes sense.

Pedro Noguera, the dean of the University of Southern California's Rossier School of Education, said that culture is about values, norms, and revealed in how people are treated every day (episode 213). He advises principals to create a culture that affirms the importance of children. Geri Parscale, an educational consultant with Solution Tree, said that culture is the way of life for that school (episode 87).

Carol Bartholomew said that powerful culture includes student voices at all levels. She's principal of a student-directed K–12 charter school in Anchorage, Alaska, where students are involved at all levels of decision making. This requires a culture that respects and accepts the contributions that students can make.

So many other guests on the *Transformative Principal* podcast have said something like, "You must change the culture before you can change anything else." These statements have always frustrated me, because when they say "change the culture" they're really saying change other things. It's never just about the culture, but because everything is so connected to the culture, you have to make room for that to change. Let's look at some more examples of what makes the culture.

Eric Chagala, principal of Vista Innovation and Design Academy (VIDA), an innovative school in Vista, California, had to completely change the culture of his school from a failing traditional school to one that used design thinking to solve real-world problems. He said, "Schools have the power to perpetuate or change the culture of the neighborhood." VIDA was in a "boring" part of the community. The homes were old, the school was old, and it wasn't considered a great place to live. So, how did he change the culture not only of his school but of his community as well? He used the design thinking process, about which I talk extensively in my book, *SchoolX* (Jones, 2020). He said that the design thinking process is all about adding value to the community and stakeholders. How could his school add value to the community, he asked? Gaining empathy is not just about trying to experience what other people are experiencing. Chagala said that in order to really understand what people need, you have to listen deeply and read between the lines.

Chagala and his staff transitioned their school from a traditional school to one based on an academic framework called design-based learning, with externships, by listening intently, and by reading between the lines. And, the powerful part is that he didn't turn over staff. The people who were there when they decided to make the change were there when the new school model was two years old.

The process he went through looked like this. Teachers would teach all day long at their old school and then spend the afternoons and evenings talking to families, listening, and gaining an understanding of what people wanted, so that when the time came, they were delivering what the families needed.

This is a big change, and it takes a lot of work to make it happen. And it requires everyone to be there on the same page, working for the same thing. If you just do a couple of things here and there, this kind of wide-scale change is not going to happen.

Going back to Pedro Noguera's definition of culture, that culture is about values and norms, and is revealed in how people are treated every day, this quote from a student at VIDA is most profound:

"Now our teachers care about us."

Trust me, you cannot walk into a school and find any teacher who doesn't care about kids. In fact, nearly every teacher out there is there for the kids. And yet, my own experience in school showed me that teachers didn't care about me. In your school right now, you likely have many students who feel like teachers don't care about them.

I lived in Russia for two years and I became fluent in Russian. It's a beautiful and challenging language. One concept that completely changed how I view education is in how they address their profession as teachers. In English, we often say, "I'm an English teacher" or "I teach high school math." In Russian, it's not possible to say that. You can make a direct translation, sure, but then it doesn't even make sense. In Russian, you say, "I teach kids to math." But let's break it down a little more. The way you would say, "I take my kids to the zoo" is the same way you say that you teach them. So, teaching in Russia is viewed as gathering kids together and taking them to a subject, rather than teaching a subject to them. This subtle difference is actually quite profound. It places the focus on the students rather than on the subject, and it empowers the teacher to put the students' needs first.

This is exactly the approach that Eric Chagala used at VIDA. Kids felt like they were the priority. But, again, you can't just do that by saying "We're focusing on culture." It's the other actions that you take that make this culture change happen.

Let's look at another school. Dr. Kimberly Miles is principal East Gresham Elementary. She was hired as a turnaround principal, and her job was to make change before the state took over the school. This is a tall order, to be sure, but it is possible, and Kimberly showed the way to make it happen.

To start, everyone had the choice to leave or apply to stay. That means that changing personnel was part of the plan from the beginning. Contrast that with Eric Chagala's school, where he didn't have a choice but to keep everyone, and still changed the culture. As Kimberly was interviewing all the teachers who applied to stay, she was looking for a willingness to do what works. To be honest, she didn't even know exactly what that was yet. She'd been a turnaround principal before, and she knew where the school struggled, but she also understood that context matters, and so she focused on a willingness to do whatever it took for the kids to be successful.

Kimberly asked the question, "How are we as a team going to fulfill the need for our kids?" What need do the kids have and how are we going to make sure it is fulfilled?

There was so much work to be done. She asked her interviewees, "Are you willing to do the work?" But people didn't know what the work was yet. This is an important piece of culture because we often don't know what we are committing to when we focus on changing culture. In fact, it is nearly impossible because so much goes into it. But Kimberly is a genius, and one of the first ways she started building a culture of change is by saying, "We GET to do this, and isn't that exciting?"

This last example where she emphasized to her teachers that we GET to do this is an example of how communication builds culture. At first, Kimberly's teachers were taken aback a bit, but as they saw her enthusiasm grow, they were able to harness that enthusiasm as well.

Another key that helped Kimberly change culture was around speed. She is a fast mover. She has an idea of where she wants to go, and she knows how to get there. She also knows that she cannot rush things too fast with her staff. She uses the mantra "go slow to go fast." She recognizes that her speed is not the same as her teachers' speed. This is a challenging concept for me, and I have asked Kimberly to explain it to me multiple times.

She explained that in order to go fast, you have to go slow. This is an old axiom that race-car drivers use. In order for a race car to go fast, there are certain parts of the course where you have to go slow. A principal can have a plethora of ideas and strategies to make things work, but dumping all of those on your teachers is not effective. They need time to get to where you are with your vision. Kimberly suggests taking a slower approach with staff. Explain the vision, so they know where they are going, but don't get bogged down in all the details just yet. Work with your team to implement the little things that lead up to the bigger ideas, rather than overwhelming them with how much there is to do. Similar to how this book is structured. Start with little things, like self-care, and before you know it, you'll be improving culture in your school by leaps and bounds.

For example, in order for achievement to rise in her school, Kimberly knew she needed effective instruction. As in any school, you can identify hundreds of ways instruction can be improved, but she didn't do that. She started with targeted professional development (PD) for her teachers around effective strategies for teaching, rather than implementing all the myriad ways they could improve. As each PD interaction proceeded, teachers were not so overwhelmed that they couldn't attain at the level that they needed to be effective. She concluded that literacy was the area to focus on. If students can read, they can do anything, so that was a good place to start. But she went even smaller and focused on a "grit and growth" mindset. These two small things can seem to take a long time to infuse in the culture of the school, and this is part of going slow to go fast.

Over time, what she found was that through targeted PD for teachers, focus on a grit and growth mindset for the students, she saw that her teachers were willing to try something new. Once they had some literacy successes, they were willing to start going faster, because the things they were learning were compounding on each other. This created a culture of feedback and trust. Teachers were willing to do the things they needed to, and Kimberly could move them faster along the path to success. Sure enough, this approach led to great improvements in literacy scores for her school, moving that once-turnaround school to the top in her district, earning three different awards in one school year.

Even in looking at these things Kimberly did to improve culture in her school, you can see that they aren't all about culture. Culture is a byproduct of the other things that we do in a school.

Identifying and Changing Culture

If we go back to Pedro Noguera's definition of culture, it is about values, norms, and how people are treated every day. Let's start by focusing on how people are treated every day. Here is a list of questions to help you identify what your culture values and prioritizes:

How are students treated when they

- Make good choices?
- Make bad choices?
- Appear invisible?
- Are absent consistently?
- Are late?
- Are on time?
- Show up consistently?
- Do their best work?
- Do the minimum work?

- Care about others?
- Don't care about others?
- Fight?
- Break rules?
- Bully?
- Stand up for bullying?
- Avoid adults?
- Avoid other kids?
- Express themselves positively?
- Express themselves in a negative way?
- Persevere?
- Give up?
- Run away from challenges?
- Greet challenges head on?
- Take control of their learning?
- Avoid work?

You can continue this line of questioning forever and with every possible behavior! You can also continue it with other roles in your school. In the questions above, replace *student* with *teacher, parent, paraprofessional, staff member,* and *principal.*

Here are a few additional questions to ask about culture for your teachers:

How do we treat teachers when they

- Treat students poorly?
- Treat students well?
- Go above and beyond?
- Do the minimum?
- Volunteer?
- Don't volunteer?
- Prioritize their responsibilities?
- Prioritize their students?
- Prioritize their content area?

Again, this list can go on and on.

Here's the important part. Just asking these questions straight up on a survey is likely not going to get the response that you are seeking.

There is too much ambiguity and opportunity for people to express what they should do or want to do, even if that isn't the case for that particular person. David Smith, from the Utah State Office of Education, encourages us to get rid of a culture of judgment and move toward a culture of improvement. Even that simple suggestion carries weight! The work we do leaves an impact on those we work with, students and teachers alike. Changing the culture of your school to be one of improvement and not of judgment is a tall order, but it is possible. Some of the cultural things we do in schools (like grades) make it hard to change that culture. If your school is giving out A–F grades, you are engaging in a culture of judgment, in that an F indicates that someone has failed.

This is a huge part of our worldwide view of life! You're not going to be able to change that in an instant.

McMinnville High School

So changing culture won't be accomplished by a survey sent out anonymously to everyone! Even though that's what we often do in education, we know it doesn't work. I've been pleased over the last several years to get to know Amy Fast, a principal at McMinnville High School in Oregon.

She's been active on Twitter since I first met her in 2015, and I invited her on the podcast the first time in 2016 (episodes 132 & 133). Amy is humble, and when I introduced her on my podcast she said, "That makes me sound a little more awesome than I am, because I'm only an assistant principal and I'm a former instructional coach and teacher."

I share this because Amy saw early on the power of what she could do, but like most transformative principals, she didn't even recognize the power she had. She shows, nearly every day on Twitter, the power of having an amazing culture in your school. She regularly shares how much she cares about her students, how hard her staff works, and how much they lift up everyone around them.

In that first interview, she spoke about how she was tasked with doing some active shooter training after a shooting at a college close to her school, and she took an unorthodox step. Instead of just talking about active shooter situations, she had a poignant thought: "There was a school shooting at a college, you know, not far away from our high school. And I just was, I just really had this need to do something that was proactive because obviously students who are feeling good about their lives don't shoot up schools, you know? So, I wanted to take an approach that was less about security and more about well-being and knowing how our students are doing."

So she asked them. Yes, in a survey, but it was not anonymous, and she followed up with every student.

She knew, early on, that culture at her school was so important, she couldn't ignore it. She not only had to address it, but also she had to get to the root level of how her kids were feeling. This led to some amazing insights, which we highlighted in chapter 6 on relationships. But more importantly, it set the tone for the kind of school she wanted to lead. She is now the principal of McMinnville High School, and her early surveys of students continue to play a role in what she is doing and how she leads her school.

Back to the early days, though. Instead of creating a form, as we are often eager to do in education, she took a different approach. She not only created the survey, but also she went to each classroom and told the kids exactly what the surveys were about. She said:

> We went into 75 different classrooms and said, you know, here's who I am. Here's what we care about. Here's what we want school to be all about.

And we care about how you're doing, and we're here to make sure that you're set up on a trajectory where you can experience joy in your learning and school can be a safe place for you to be in a place where you feel connected to people and feel like you matter. We want to get this information from you because we want to do right by you. And you know, all the time we sit in these back rooms as adults and we make decisions about how to do right by you and how to help you on your trajectory. And we never asked you, and you know more than anyone. So, we're asking you today. And so please be honest. And even though the survey is not anonymous, it is completely confidential. And you can say what you want to say. You have free rein, so here's your chance.

Instead of sending out an anonymous survey, she went to every classroom and told the kids about the survey, and she told them she would read it all and follow up. She had several people working together to codify the results. And then she called the kids into the office, bought pizza, and said, "Hey, what can we do? This is horrible. You guys aren't feeling connected and I'm sorry. And why is that?"

Perhaps one of the best indicators that this approach was working came in the form of a comment from a student in the hallway. Amy describes it: "And she goes, 'Hey, I just wanted to thank you for what you guys are doing with this student survey.' She said, 'All my friends and I have been talking about it and, and we didn't realize that administrators even remembered what it was like to be teenagers. And it's pretty cool what you're doing. And do you mind if I give you a hug?'"

Is there connection in that school now? You bet there is. And this lays the groundwork for powerful relationships that can make things happen that you wouldn't normally get if you are just managing a school. This is what transformative principals do, and Amy is a great example of that.

Multicultural

At this point, we are going to change our approach on culture to multi-culture, which is respecting and honoring the cultures of the people in your school. As we've mentioned before, culture is how people are treated on a daily basis, and this is often more important than we think. Over the last couple of years, there has been a lot of talk on anti-racist teaching, critical race theory, and so much more. How we treat people of different cultures is a part of what makes the culture in our schools.

I am certainly not an expert on many of these issues, but I have interviewed people who are.

I have a deep spiritual belief that we are all children of God. Whether or not you also believe this, it's a good place to start. Sometimes, I use the idea that we are all human beings. Before anyone is Black, White, Filipino, Kenyan, Christian, Buddhist, Catholic, Jewish, or anything else, they are first children of God and, as such, should be treated as individuals who matter and have divine potential. This deep spiritual belief has served me greatly over the years because it immediately gives me respect for whatever else is added to that initial truth and it always gives us a starting place for common beliefs.

This approach was affirmed by Dr. Sebrina Lindsay-Law (episode 419), Coordinator for Equity and Opportunity in the Office for Diversity, Equity, and Inclusion for Virginia Beach City Public Schools. Her advice to anyone striving to be more inclusive is to start with humanity. We have to recognize that we have way more in common than we think.

We all have biases, and we have all had previous interactions with people from different cultures that influence how we perceive them. From my own life, growing up in Southern California, my high school had Native American and Mexican students who had ongoing conflicts with each other. One of the defining moments of my high school career was the feeling in the air as seemingly "every" Mexican and Native American student was heading to the football field for a huge fight. I headed the other way to not be anywhere near that! Another defining moment was when many Mexican students, staff, and allies walked out of school when Proposition 187 was up for a vote in California "to make immigrants residing in the country without legal permission ineligible for public benefits" (Ballotpedia, 1994). To be honest, at that time I didn't know what it meant, but I experienced this while in high school and it made an impact on me.

These experiences shape who we are. Rather than fear them, bury them, or reinforce the negative experiences, we should seek to understand them.

Sebrina encourages people to not bury their biases and pretend they don't exist, but rather to be aware of them and then judge them. Our experiences and biases make us who we are, and asking ourselves to change who we are just to fit in is just as bad as asking someone to change who they are to fit in. To be clear, Sebrina was not saying that you should continue in your biases that put people down and cause you to treat them poorly. She was clearly stating that you need to be your authentic self. The biases exist but they can't rule our lives; nor can we pretend they don't exist. We need to be constantly defining ourselves. She suggests that you should be personable according to your own style.

Stephen MR Covey in Speed of Trust describes authenticity this way: "A person has integrity when there is no gap between intent and behavior . . . when he or she is whole, seamless, the same—inside and out. This kind of authenticity is what I call "congruence." And it is congruence—not compliance—that will ultimately create credibility and trust." (Covey, p. 64).

Tracey Ezard, in her book *Ferocious Warmth* describes authenticity this way: "My ability to lead is based on connection and collaboration with others. I let others see both my vulnerability and courage through authentic relationships. I use power to make the world a better place. I am who you see."

Sometimes, as I think of these early experiences I have had, I can become uncomfortable about what I am feeling, as I am sure you do sometimes, as well. Sebrina encourages us to be comfortable with discomfort.

One area that is particularly difficult is that we as educators like things wrapped up and complete, but it isn't always possible for that to happen. Sebrina invites us to be "more receptive to non-closure." She explains that it is okay to end a conversation, especially as it relates to diversity, equity, and inclusion, without having every aspect answered. This can be very challenging for us! Sometimes, we need to leave those conversations open-ended, even if it feels uncomfortable. It's okay to not have all the answers in that moment.

We need to find those things that make us different and use them to help us be unified and inclusive. This can be counterintuitive, but by recognizing that others have skills, abilities, and dispositions that we don't, we can use those differences to help us build on common ground.

Clare Fulp (episode 174) is the principal of Chugach Optional school in Chugach, Alaska. Each summer, she runs a program for refugee students in and around Anchorage, Alaska. In changing the program from one that focused only on hiring English language learner (ELL) teachers and getting them into the classrooms, Clare made the focus more about serving the students in a particular way: "language-rich environments through super high engagement."

The culture previously was all about structured programs with ELL support. Now the structure is about kids learning everywhere. Clare said,

"Kids do math down the hallway, measuring things…we're using every nook and cranny and it's not like you're confined to one specific area. So, the physical space is so key for any school. And now that I've been at Chugach, there's so much more light in the kids' lives and adult lives with just the sunshine coming in and then being exposed to other learning environments. It's really quite amazing."

Sometimes, in our efforts to "raise everyone up," we don't give the same experiences to our students from nondominant cultures. Clare emphasizes that you have to work hard to make it happen for all students, not just those who fit the mold. For more on that, please check out my other book, *SchoolX* (Jones, 2020).

Dr. Kara Four Bear (episodes 108 and 109) is an administrator in New Town, North Dakota, where her student population is largely Native American like her. She dropped out of high school and eventually achieved a doctoral degree. Every day, she asks kids what they want to be when they grow up, and she always suggests they go into teaching (smart move, by the way). She said that they respond with something like, "I never thought of myself having a job, let alone being a teacher. Could I really do that?" For her student population to have never thought of having a job, it's a pretty remarkable situation. She loves encouraging kids to think beyond their environment, and said, "I'm just imagining their inner dialogues by reading their faces. And I just get a kick out of it. It's great to see their eyes light up … So, I guess being the teacher that you would want being their champion and then pushing them in the right direction, planting those seeds." This is exactly what Kara is doing—she's helping her students see a future for themselves that is different than what they envision.

Too often our approach to multiculturalism is to try to make everyone like us. My dad used to say something to me that in my youth I never really understood. He said, "Jethro, I hope you are better than me in every way." I never understood that. I always thought, "Don't you want to be better, yourself, Dad?"

Well, I realize now that he did want to be better, but more important, he wanted me to be better than him. He didn't want me to struggle with the things he struggled with, and he inspired me to be better. Too often, our expectation is for kids to just graduate or just get a job. We need to be more like Kara and Clare, who have expectations about the people our youth become, not only about what they do.

We need to be kids' champions and help them achieve what they are most certainly capable of.

Zaretta Hammond (episodes 156–157) explained this best when she said that kids can't learn from people they don't trust. In order for them to learn from us, they need to trust us. And kids are pretty good at knowing whom to trust and whom not to trust. She said, "The reason that you're building trust is connected to the brain science. We can't learn if we're stressed out. We can't learn if we are not feeling supported or we're feeling distrustful. So, if we know teachers are already saying things to us that make us feel inadequate," then we've lost their trust.

She talks about "trust generators," which are powerful ways to build trust quickly. One such trust generator is selective vulnerability. "What that means is I tell you something about myself that reveals kind of the inner me. And in return, we usually will reveal something about ourselves in return. And that whole process actually creates oxytocin in our brains, which binds us, so that we feel more trusting and less stress. And we're more likely to hang in there when there's a conflict, because we feel friendly with that person."

She then told a story of an eighth-grade teacher, and one of the things she did to build the selective vulnerability. She taped a picture of herself as an eighth grader to her front desk.

"And the students were like, oh my gosh, that was you in eighth grade! I mean, it was all her in all her eighth-grade glory, braces and all. And she said, yes. And as they saw that, wow, now this is who you are, right now: a capable, attractive woman. I possibly can be that and the fact that she would be that vulnerable with them, they made themselves more vulnerable, their willingness to share their struggles. And this started to bond them individually with her, but also collectively as a classroom with each other, as they then were actually starting to build trust."

Zaretta mentions several other trust generators in her book, *Culturally Responsive Teaching and the Brain*. Many of the strategies mentioned in this book also contribute to those trust generators, which makes it easier to find success in building trust with students and with faculty.

The whole topic of diversity, equity, and inclusion is an uncomfortable one for most people, because it is uncomfortable to confront the challenges that we all face, especially in education where we are expected to be perfect all the time.

Culture is so important, but you can see in this chapter that when I'm talking about culture, I'm really still talking about all the other things that we do. This is so important I have to keep emphasizing it. Diversity, equity, and inclusion is not about critical race theory or affirmative action or immigration or anything else. It's about how we treat the people in our schools. And we need to start with the things we have in common, and *build* from there, not tear down.

If you're doing it right...

If you're implementing this book how I suggest, in that you start with the small dominoes and build from there, by the time you start thinking about culture, you will have already laid all the groundwork, and the positive culture that exists in your school will be a noticeable outcome of the work you have done in all the other areas. It's like magic.

So, to be honest, this can really be a simple chapter to implement, because the culture is made up of all the other things that you will have done previously. Those trust generators will make the culture in the building powerful.

Sometimes, you'll just see that there are great things that are happening in your culture that you couldn't have planned for. Bryan Hyosaka (episode 428) teaches at a micro school in Denver, Colorado. It are located in a bicycle shop and a coffee shop. It's a pretty unique environment, and he said something profound. After some kids created a new flavor of latte as a learning opportunity and as a contest, it ended up selling very well. Bryan reflected on the culture there: "One of the greatest markers, I think, of the culture that we have here among the losing groups, even, was they probably have bought more of the lemon lavender latte than any other customer in the general public. And so, there is no resentment or hostility. They're very happy for their classmates because intimately they know how hard those other groups worked. It speaks to the culture, and maybe that's a micro school thing, I'm not quite sure. It really does say that they get it."

It's not just a micro school thing. When the culture in a school is healthy, supportive, and a place where people want to be themselves, it's really powerful. Transformative principals create that culture by all the other little things they do.

Chapter Summary

"For, if the culture of our schools affects the character of our pupils, and the character of our pupils then eventually shapes the culture of our society, undoubtedly what we teach our pupils does make a genuine difference to the world around us." This quote is from Katharine Birbalsingh (episode 368), head of school at Michaela Community School in London.

What we teach our students, not only through bookwork, but also through our example and the "unspoken curriculum" matters greatly.

The culture that exists in your school is the result of your efforts. It's your fault! The good news about that is you can fix it. You can fix it by doing little things that lead up to it.

Key Questions

1. What are the things you can do to effectively improve your school's culture?
2. How can you know how people really feel in your school?
3. What is the big takeaway you have from learning about culture?
4. When was the last time you felt truly safe to be authentic in your work?
5. What will you do to be truly authentic going forward?

References

Ballotpedia. (1994). California proposition 187, prohibit undocumented immigrants from using public healthcare, schools, and social services initiative (1994). https://ballotpedia.org/California_Proposition_187,_Illegal_Aliens_Ineligible_for_Public_Benefits_

Covey, S. M.R. (2006). The SPEED of Trust: The One Thing that Changes Everything (p. 117). Free Press. Kindle Edition.

Ezard, T. (2021). Ferocious Warmth - School Leaders Who Inspire and Transform (p. 54). Tracey Ezard Pty Ltd. Kindle Edition.

Hammond, Z. L. (2015). Culturally responsive teaching and the brain: Promoting authentic engagement and rigor among culturally and linguistically diverse students. Corwin.

Jones, J. (2020). SchoolX: How principals can design a transformative school experience for students, teachers, parents—and themselves. John Catt.

Lencioni, P. M. (2012). *The advantage: Why organizational health trumps everything else in business.* Jossey-Bass.

Quinn, R. E. (1996). *Deep change: Discovering the leader within.* Jossey-Bass.

Endnotes

Listen to the podcast

You can find the podcast anywhere you find podcasts. It's on every platform I can get it on. Let me know if you can't find it. Just search for Transformative Principal anywhere, and as it is the longest running school leadership podcast out there, you'll be able to find it easily.

A note about listening to specific episodes of the podcast. There is so much great content. At the time of publication, I've just surpassed 450 "official" episodes of the Transformative Principal podcast. There have been over a million downloads and if you listen to them all straight through, it would take days. To be honest, it's pretty much impossible to condense all of that in a book, but I'm doing my best here.

To find any episode where you know the episode number (which I provide throughout the book) just go to https://transformativeprincipal. org/episode### and enter the number. There are not leading zeroes, so if you want to go way back to episode 23, it is https://transformativeprincipal. org/episode23.

If you remember a person's name, you can easily find them by typing their name in the search box which I renamed to "Who do you want to learn from"? If you're nerdy like me, you can just enter this url: https://www.transformativeprincipal.org/?s=FirstName+LastName and you'll be able to find someone that way also. So if you want to hear my episode with Todd Whitaker, you would enter https://www. transformativeprincipal.org/?s=todd+whitaker. Capitalizing doesn't matter, but don't use spaces.